SIR ROBERT PEEL'S
ADMINISTRATION
1841-1846

PEEL'S CHEAP BREAD SHOP,
OPENED JANUARY 22, 1846.

SIR ROBERT PEEL'S ADMINISTRATION

1841-1846

Travis L. Crosby

DAVID & CHARLES   *Newton Abbot*
                 London   Vancouver
ARCHON BOOKS   *Hamden   Connecticut*
1976

Library of Congress Cataloging in Publication Data

Crosby, Travis L   1936-
    Sir Robert Peel's administration, 1841-1846.

    Bibliography: p.
    Includes index.
    1. Great Britain—Politics and government
—1837-1901. 2.   Great Britain—Economic
policy. 3. Great   Britain—Social   policy. I.
Title.
D. ₅550.C68   1976   320.9′41′081   76-927

© Travis L. Crosby 1976

Published in Great Britain by David &
Charles (Holdings) Ltd, Newton Abbot, Devon, and in the United States
of America as an Archon Book, an im-
print of The Shoe String Press, Inc.,
Hamden, Connecticut 06514

ISBN 0 7153 7159 2 (*Great Britain*)
ISBN 0-208-01517-5 (*United States*)

Set in eleven on thirteen point Times
Roman and printed in the United States
of America by Cushing-Malloy Inc.
Ann Arbor, Michigan

Contents

Acknowledgements

I am grateful in the first instance to Michael Hurst who suggested that I should write this book. There are many others who eased my path and made my task a pleasurable one. Among them are the staff and librarians of the Manuscript Room and Newspaper Collection of the British Museum, the Public Record Office, the University of London Library, the Institute of Historical Research, the Cambridge University Library, the National Trust at Hughenden, and the Harvard University Library. Lord Blake very kindly allowed me access to the Derby Manuscripts at Queen's College, Oxford. I am especially grateful to those who willingly burdened themselves with reading and criticising the manuscript: they are Richard W. Davis, Norman Gash, and my colleague, Jane E. Ruby. They will understand if I did not follow their thoughtful suggestions in every case.

I should also like to thank Wheaton College for sabbatical leave to complete this book, and the Wheaton College Faculty Research Fund for financial assistance. My thanks, too, for the typing services of Wheaton's long-suffering faculty secretary, Mrs Nancy Shepardson.

A special note of thanks and appreciation I should like to give to two others. Faye Crosby took time from her busy schedule to peruse numerous poll books diligently, accurately, and enthusiastically. She has also read the manuscript, insisting more often than I would like to admit on clarity and precision. To our son, Matthew, whose birth coincided with the final stages of the book, I am grateful for quiet moments at crucial times, and for happy diversions at other times. To him the book is dedicated.

Introduction

The discussion of a single political administration has a certain advantage: it allows concentration and depth. One may gain a more detailed understanding of statesmen at work. But there is a concomitant disadvantage: concentration on a single administration may lead the historian to claim too much. Such a temptation is especially great in the case of the administration of Sir Robert Peel. His reputation, already established, has been enhanced by a recent (and probably definitive) biography.[1] Peel's parliamentary skills, prodigious industry, and administrative talents were unmatched and well recognised in his own day. Yet Peel did not enjoy complete success. His record on social reform was spotty. He seemed insensitive to some of the broader political movements of the day. And his relations with his political party, never easy, broke down completely in 1846 and led the Conservatives to twenty years in the political wilderness. Part of our task is to account for Peel's failures as well as for his successes.

The essential aim for Peel's administration was to promote an orderly economic growth while mitigating the harmful social consequences of industrialisation. In the early decades of the industrial revolution, the potential for growth seemed unlimited as the factory system and technological innovation enormously increased productive capacity. Agricultural improvements had a similar effect upon the land. During the Napoleonic Wars, industrial output and extensive agriculture were both encouraged by the government to meet wartime exigencies. The great question after 1815, however, was whether the new industrial system could sustain its growth in peacetime. The record to 1841 was inconclusive but not encouraging. There was a short, sharp depression in 1815 immediately after the Napoleonic Wars. Recovery and further expansion throughout much of the 1820s and early 1830s only presaged a critical depression in the late 1830s and early 1840s. The year 1842 is generally regarded as the nadir of that depression, and as perhaps the most depressed of the nineteenth century. A similar cycle of expansion and depression may be seen in agriculture: a postwar slump, followed by a brief revival in the 1820s and a further slump in the 1830s.

Generally speaking, overproduction lay at the root of the difficulty.[2] Excess productive capacity in cotton, wool, and iron on the industrial side was matched by abundant grain harvests on the agricultural side. This led to a decline in investment, discontinued production, reduced wages, and ultimately widespread unemployment among workers. Indeed, to twentieth-century eyes, the unemployment levels were staggering. For example, the number of unemployed in Bolton in 1842 among bricklayers was 87 percent, among carpenters 84 percent, among mill workers 60 percent, among stonemasons, tailors, and shoemakers 50 percent. In Liverpool, slightly less than half the shoemakers and slightly more than half the tailors were unemployed. Such figures were common throughout the distressed regions in Britain.[3] Exacerbating this cyclical unemployment of craftsmen and factory operatives was the steadily growing number of the technologically unemployed among the domestic outworkers, such as the handloom weavers and the framework knitters. For these practitioners of a dying trade, the cyclical downturn was disastrous. The effect of massive unemployment was reflected in the system of poor relief. In 1842, 20 percent of the working population of Nottingham were on poor relief; 33 percent of Paisley depended on charity.[4] In Leicester, some 5,000 persons, ten times the capacity of the workhouse, were receiving relief during the winter of 1841-2.[5] In Sheffield five times as much was spent on outdoor as on indoor paupers in 1842.[6]

Wages and security of employment were not the only grievances among working-class Britons. Conditions of life and work were far from satisfactory. Within the factories, excessive hours, unfenced machinery, overheated and dirty air were fatiguing and dangerous. Life outside the factories in the industrial cities was scarcely better. Although historians debate the rate of increase in real wages between 1790 and 1840, there seems more agreement that the quality of life was deteriorating. Overcrowding, insanitary housing, and a polluted environment were not only everyday discomforts; they bred the common diseases of typhus and tuberculosis which ensured a short lifespan for the town-dwelling workman. Indeed, in the first decades of the nineteenth century there was a real increase in the national death rate over previous decades.[7]

The grim conditions of working-class life and the dissatisfaction it provoked among working-class Britons posed a serious challenge to governments of the day. The threat to social order was considerable: unemployed workers often struck out erratically and violently by riot and arson in the traditional manner of the downtrodden. Understandably, the fear of revolutionary upheaval was never far from the minds of governments of the 1830s and 1840s. Groups of working-class agitators lent credence to this fear by flying the tricolour or adopting the slogans of the French Revolution at protest meetings. This has led some historians to believe that the working class was on the verge of revolt in these distressed decades. But the existence of what one historian has called 'the language of menace' did not necessarily indicate revolutionary intentions.[8] Middle-class radicals, for instance, had consciously used the threat of revolution as a tactic to force concessions from the government during the reform agitations of the early 1830s. There was no intention of carry-

ing out such a threat: the inculcation of a 'wholesome
terror' was considered sufficient. It seems likely that working-class agitators adopted the same tactics. They were not
revolutionaries so much as meliorists, working for the improvement rather than the destruction of existing institutions. To that end, they organised national movements
aiming to persuade Parliament to redress their grievances
through legislation. This was a significant episode in the
politics of public opinion. It indicated the growing aware-
ness among working men of the potential strength of the
'associative principle'.

To governments of the day, working-class organisations
designed to put pressure on Parliament were more threatening than random acts of violence, since they represented a
dangerous extension of the practice of public petitioning.[9]
Throughout most of the eighteenth century, the only legitimate petitioning was that through official channels—from
established institutions such as municipal corporations or
universities, or from special meetings, such as county meetings, convened to petition for specific grievances. Even
through these channels, there was little that might be called
political petitioning. In the late eighteenth century, however,
a series of events beginning with the Wilkes affair and later
the disasters of the American war established the respecta-
bility of political petitioning. Philanthropic groups such as
Wilberforce's anti-slavery movement also took up the device.
The turmoil of the Napoleonic Wars slowed the growth of
these extra-parliamentary groups. After 1815, however, they
revived in full vigour. The Catholic Association and the
various political unions of the 1830s were among the most
active. The working-class organisations of the 1830s and
1840s were in the tradition of these pressure groups. Parliament had never welcomed the development of the extra-
parliamentary tradition, for it implied the existence of a
higher authority outside Parliament. Once the working
class had adopted the politics of extra-parliamentary agita-

tion after 1815, the implication was even more repugnant: bowing to their demands would come dangerously near to legitimising democratic procedure.

Perhaps more than any other in the nineteenth century, Peel's administration was faced with the full brunt of agitating working-class movements. The three great movements of the 1830s—factory reform, the anti-Poor Law campaign, and Chartism—retained their appeal among working men in the 1840s. That the 'associative principle' had extended very far among working men was further illustrated in 1842 with the so-called Plug Plot, during which striking colliers organised massive demonstrations against wage reductions. These working-class movements had only slight success in achieving their aims. They were too ineffectively led, too loosely brought together, and never long sustained by unity of purpose. But they revealed dramatically the high social costs of industrialising society, and they posed exceptional difficulties for the Peel administration.

Not all movements of the 1840s were concerned with working-class grievances. The striking fact of the early 1840s is the unusual number and variety of popular movements, including the Irish repeal movement, the Rebecca Riots, the Anti-Corn Law League, and the Anti-League. These are less easy to characterise than the working-class movements, for they had quite different, even antagonistic, aims. Potentially the most explosive was the Irish repeal agitation, for it linked religion and nationality in such a way as to ensure a unity of purpose that would be the envy of any popular movement. Celtic dissatisfaction was not limited to Ireland, as the Rebecca Riots indicated. In the three counties of remote West Wales the complaints of nonconformist small farmers about high rents, an arbitrary magistracy, and Anglican rates and tithes burst into prominence in late 1842 with a series of threatening nocturnal demonstrations and destruction of property. Perhaps the best-known of all the movements of the 1840s was the Anti-Corn Law League. From its

origins in Manchester in 1838, the League became a well-
financed and well-organised nationwide campaign within
a few years, espousing the virtues of free trade to every part
of the country. Self-consciously middle-class, the League
believed free trade would be the corrosive to end aristocratic
dominance. Not surprisingly, it antagonised the protectionists of the landed interest. Farmers especially, goaded by the
League's countryside campaign, organised themselves
against the advance of free-trade doctrine, and established
the Anti-League in 1843; it soon spread throughout the
counties.

The task of Peel's administration in seeking to balance the
claims of these various pressure groups and to ease the dis-
content that lay behind them was a difficult one. How could
the ministry reconcile the conflicting claims of manufacturing free traders, landed protectionists, and working-class
reformers? Equally serious from the ministry's point of view
was the threat to social order posed by these groups. Were
boisterous meetings of Chartists or Leaguers, with inflam-
matory harangues, to be tolerated? A ministry too concerned with order might well mistake noisy demonstrations
of opinion for seditious utterances. Peel's ministry did have
a tendency to disallow expressions 'out of doors' as manifestations of legitimate interest. It did not, however, react
as Lord Liverpool's had during similar disturbances in
1815-20, when Habeas Corpus was suspended, the sedition
laws strengthened, and a series of treason trials begun. None-
theless, the Peel ministry used magistrates, police, and military forces to the full when dealing with riot and disorder,
ignoring less violent manifestations of dissent. Such a policy
had its strengths as well as its weaknesses; essentially a
policy of moderation, it contributed to the reputation of the
ministry for firmness, lending credence to its public statements of intention to preserve the peace. Yet, paradoxically,
the ministry's unwillingness to come to terms with extra-

parliamentary agitation may have led to greater frustration among dissatisfied groups and hence to greater agitation.

The growth of organised pressure groups in society was indicative of a growing selfconsciousness, not merely of economic interests, but of religious, philanthropic, and political interests as well. Each interest was becoming more skilled in placing its claim before Parliament. By the mid-nineteenth century, the clash of numerous well-organised contending interests was loud enough to force any government of the day to hear, if not to heed, their demands. The growth of these extra-parliamentary instruments of opinion was bound to have an effect upon electoral politics when interest groups broadened their activities from petitioning to political campaigns at election time. Parliamentary elections were no longer merely a market where votes were bought and sold. Issues and party platforms were matters of concern to an increasingly sophisticated electorate. The election of 1841 may serve as an example.

SIR ROBERT PEEL'S
ADMINISTRATION
1841-1846

THE MODERN SISYPHUS.

"Sisyphus is said to be doomed for ever to roll to the top of a great mountain a stone, which continually falls down again."

Sisyphus . . Sir R. P—l.   The Stone .   D. O'C—l.   The Furies . .   Lord J. R—l, S—l, &c.

1 THE ELECTION
AND THE NEW MINISTRY

The general election of 1841, which brought Sir Robert Peel
to power, confirmed the revival of Conservative party
fortunes since 1832. In 1832, the Conservatives had won
only 185 of 658 parliamentary seats: in 1841, they won 367
of 658. The Conservatives enjoyed their greatest success in
the English counties. Winning only 42 of 144 county seats
in 1832, they won 124 in 1841. Representatives of great
Whig county families such as Lords Morpeth and Milton in
the West Riding, Lord Howick in North Northumberland,
Sir Charles Cavendish in East Sussex, and the Earl of Sur-
rey in West Sussex went down to defeat. Never again would
the Conservatives do as well in the counties. The Conservatives also won some surprising victories in the English
boroughs, including one seat at Leeds and two of the four
seats of the City of London. From only 83 of 323 English
borough seats in 1832, the Conservatives increased their total
to 155 in 1841. The Conservatives also won a majority of
Welsh seats in 1841, 19 of the 29 total; and a slight Conservative trend was felt in Scotland and Ireland, although it was
not enough to offset the overwhelming Whig advantage: the
Conservatives won 22 of 53 Scottish seats and 43 of 105
Irish.

Predictably, some Whig spokesmen blamed Conservative
bribery for their defeat: 'every engine of corruption and op-
pression' of the Conservatives had been set to work during
the election, claimed the *Morning Chronicle*.[1] As predictably, the Conservatives declared that the election results could
be explained by a genuine conversion to Conservative beliefs.

The truth lay somewhere in between these partisan claims. Bribery there was, but not enough to account for such a Conservative victory. In any case, the Whigs themselves were not free from this electoral practice. A Conservative sentiment in the country did exist, but it was more a temporary reaction to the Whig policies of a decade than evidence of a permanent Whig decline.

The weakness of the Whig administration was obvious by 1841. In power almost continuously since 1830, the Whigs had alienated various sections of the electorate over the years. Radical support was forfeited by a distinct cooling of the once-ardent Whig reformist spirit. Among the propertied classes, there was dissatisfaction with the Whig inability to prevent the riots and disorder of the late 1830s. There was also among the electorate at large a growing doubt about the fiscal and administrative capacity of the Whigs. As economic distress deepened, the Whig budget deficit had mounted proportionately. By 1841, it had reached £6 million, with no solution in sight. Furthermore, some of the electorate were unhappy with the pro-Irish policy of the Whigs. When the Whigs entered into an informal political alliance in 1835 with Daniel O'Connell, leader of the Irish party, they were doubly damned for consorting with both Irishmen and Catholics. Although it is unlikely that anti-popery in 1841 won to the Conservatives many who had not already been won by other considerations, there is little doubt that O'Connell was generally unpopular in England.

The general disenchantment with Whig policies found expression during the election campaign in two major campaign issues, tariff reform and the new Poor Law. Tariff revision appears to be the more important of the two. The Whig cabinet, forced by their fiscal difficulties to find additional revenue, had decided in the spring of 1841 to lower import duties on timber, sugar, and corn. This, they hoped, would encourage the consumption of those goods, and thus secure additional revenue from increased imports. Reduction of the duties on corn imports was a project especially dear to the heart of the Colonial Secretary, Lord John Russell, who had urged it upon the cabinet for more than two years. By attacking the protectionist corn law, Lord John may also have hoped for political support from the industrial free-trade boroughs should the scheme be rejected by the House of Commons, necessitating an election.

On 30 April 1841, the Chancellor of the Exchequer, Sir Francis Baring, revealed in his budget the details of the proposed tariff revision.[2] He suggested raising the duty on imported colonial timber from 10s to 20s per load (50 cubic feet), but lowering it on foreign timber by 5s to 50s per load. This would equalise somewhat the Baltic and (hitherto more favoured) Canadian timber imports. Secondly, Baring proposed retaining the duty on colonial sugar imports at 24s per cwt while reducing it dramatically on foreign sugar imports—from 63s to 36s per cwt. Again the effect would be to equalise imports. Brazil might now compete more readily with the traditional colonial suppliers in the West Indies. Even with the revision of the sugar and timber duties, however, there remained a deficit of some £400,000. This would be made up by abolishing the sliding scale (as established by the Corn Law of 1828) and replacing it with a moderate fixed duty on corn.

The budget offered the Conservatives a number of targets, for it struck simultaneously at the shipping, West Indian, colonial timber, and agricultural interests. After a series of strategy sessions, they decided to make sugar the main line of attack. It was, as the *Manchester Guardian* noted on 12 May 1841 a 'crafty' move, for it allowed the Conservatives to bring a moral tone to their opposition. They could argue that the reduction of foreign sugar import duties might encourage the continuance of slavery in countries such as Brazil and Cuba which would be likely to increase their slave labour force to meet the demands of the British market. The Conservatives, by adopting this approach, would have the additional advantage of securing support from the powerful anti-slavery groups outside Parliament. Peel had revealed the anti-slavery argument as a Conservative tactic when he criticised in the House of Commons Baring's intention to introduce 'slave-grown sugar' into Britain. Such an act, he said, might jeopardise 'the progress of the great experiment now going on as regards the production of free labour.'[3]

Debate in the House of Commons on the Whig proposals began on 7 May and lasted eight evenings. In addition to their criticism of the sugar duties, the Conservatives attacked the perilous Whig fiscal position. The most memorable contribution to the debate was made by Peel himself on the final night. After criticising the budgetary deficits, Peel asked the House, to the delight of his supporters: 'Can there be a more lamentable picture than that of a Chancellor of the Exchequer seated on an empty chest—by the pool of a bottomless deficiency—fishing for a Budget?'[4] Peel's rhetorical question found a ready answer in the division lobby: the Whigs were in a minority of thirty-six. Their ministerial days were numbered. On 7 June, the Whigs lost a no-confidence motion by a single vote, 312–311. Even the desperate expedient of carrying into the division lobby the unconscious Lord Douglas Hallyburton, reputed to be in a state of idiocy, had not saved the Whigs. Elections were set for 28 June: they lasted until 17 July.

The general election of 1841 was the first in which the government of the day, previously holding a majority in the House of Commons, was defeated by a disciplined opposition organised for electoral purposes.[5] The election thus witnessed an important development in party organisation. It was a direct response to the growth of public opinion and an informed electorate outside Parliament. To capture that opinion, the political parties had to cast their platforms in as attractive a manner as possible. Because of their disastrous defeat in 1832, the Conservatives had been forced to re-examine their electoral strategy more carefully than the Whigs, whose comfortable (albeit declining) parliamentary majorities throughout the 1830s had lulled them into a false sense of security. Conservative agents such as F. R. Bonham and party leaders such as Sir James Graham brought unusual dedication and skill to electioneering.

This is not to say that the election of 1841 was fought wholly on the plane of party platforms. As in decades past, corrupt practices (bribery, treating, and intimidation) were widely exercised. The most flagrant example of bribery during the election was at Sudbury, Suffolk, which was later disfranchised by Parliament for its corruption. Influence, as distinct from corrupt practices, was also unquestionably exerted. This included the exercise of patronage and power by the traditional sources—the government of the day, the court, and the borough magnates—upon the constituencies. In addition, there were instances of candidates promising special benefits to the electors for their votes. Ashburton (Devon), apparently turned to the Whig candidate in 1841 because of his association with a shipping firm likely to revive a faltering China trade.[6] At Newcastle-under-Lyme (Staffs), a centre of hat manufacturing, the feltmakers gave substantial support to an untried Whig candidate, a hatmaker from Southwark who promised that, should he be elected, 'they would never be short of work.'[7]

Without a more detailed examination of virtually every local contest, however, it is impossible to determine precisely the extent of corruption and influence in 1841. There is growing evidence that the electorate as a whole may have been less swayed by corruption and influence than once was thought.[8] Certainly in 1841 circumstances disinclined the electorate to take their political opinions at second hand. Uneasy social and economic conditions prompted voters to look carefully at the political alternatives. They were of a mind to be wooed. The Conservatives wooed them. The discussion which follows emphasises Conservative electoral tactics during the election.

The borough elections were held first. The Whigs hoped to reverse the recent Conservative trend in the boroughs with their tariff revision scheme which held out to urban consumers the promise of cheaper bread and sugar. But it seems that tariff revision was not enough to offset the soiled reputation of Whig financial policies. The opinion of *The Times* that the Whigs were 'a set of reckless financial empirics' was very likely widely held.[9] During the campaign, Conservative candidates made much of the timing of tariff revision, attacking it as a 'panic budget' and suggesting that it was politically motivated. This seems to have had its effect. As the diarist Greville noted at the close of the borough elections:

> The Whigs complain bitterly of the apathy and indifference that have prevailed, and cannot recover from their surprise that their promises of cheap bread and cheap sugar have not proved more attractive.[10]

In addition to denouncing the tariff revision in general terms as an example of Whig financial irresponsibility, the Conservatives also brought protectionist pressure to bear on the boroughs. The smaller boroughs were especially susceptible to this kind of pressure. With only a few hundred voters in many instances, the smaller boroughs served as centres of general supply for the surrounding rural trade, and there was often a strong community of interest between them and the countryside. Their customers included the farmers and gentry who lived within a convenient market radius. For the most part protectionists, the farmers and gentry opposed any alteration in the Corn Law and no doubt made their opinions known to the tradesmen of their respective boroughs. Altogether, of the 202 smaller boroughs (defined as less than 1,000 electors), the Conservatives won 111—an increase of 13 over 1837.[11]

In the larger cathedral, market, or county towns, the Conservatives' stand on tariff reform may have worked to their advantage for the same reason. Of these middling-sized boroughs (between 1,000 and 2,000 electors), the Conservatives gained three seats for a total of twenty-nine.[12] Like smaller boroughs, some of these middling boroughs often served an important rural market. The shopkeeping and artisan electorate might well be uncertain how their customers from the surrounding countryside would be affected by Corn Law reduction. Conservative candidates played on this uncertainty. At Reading, for example, where two Conservatives were returned for the first time in forty years, the Conservative candidate Charles Russell reminded an election crowd of the importance of its rural customers: 'Living in a great measure by this great agricultural market, what will become of you the tradesmen and artisans of Reading, if your neighbours and friends, the landowners and farmers, are ruined?'[13] The same tactic was used at Cambridge. There, a Conservative speaker noted the importance to the town of the University, and how much of its income was derived from land. An alteration of the Corn Laws might affect that income, he declared. Should the Whigs go so far as to repeal the Corn Laws, University income could, he assured his audience, go down 'one third'.[14]

The effectiveness of such tactics is difficult to determine, but the poll books of both Reading and Cambridge indicate that tradesmen and artisans did not vote as heavily for the Whigs as might have been expected.[15] At Reading, carpenters voted Whig by only 23–20; shoemakers, 22–20; tailors, 18–16, and grocers actually favoured the Conservatives by 26–25. This allowed the more Conservative groups— such as butchers (10–6) and gentlemen (56–38)—to carry the day.[16] At Cambridge, Whig supporters voted less heavily in 1841 than in 1835 for their candidates. Grocers, for example, who supported the leading Whig by 21–12 over the trailing Conservative in 1835 voted only 23–18 for the Whigs

over the Conservatives in straight party voting in 1841. Shoemakers, who had voted 33–16 for the leading Whig over the
Conservative in 1835, voted only 31–28 for the Whigs in 1841.
The result was that two Conservative candidates were returned for Cambridge, reversing the 1837 decision.[17] These
limited statistics can obviously only be suggestive since occupational homogeneity in voting patterns has yet to be
proved conclusively.[18] But there is no doubt of the increased
Conservative support among those occupational groups
which had previously given a larger proportion of their votes
to the Whigs.

In the largest boroughs (above 2,000 electors), however,
the Whigs had more success: they gained two seats from the
Conservatives.[19] But even among these boroughs, tariff
revision was not always viewed favourably. In Liverpool,
for example, where there were strong ties with the Canadian
timber trade, the Whig intention of raising the duty on
Canadian timber was viewed with alarm. At a meeting of
the shipwrights' society of Liverpool, a spokesman declared
that the discouragement of the North American timber
trade would ruin the Liverpool shipping interest.[20] Since
the Liverpool docking and shipping interest had traditionally
given the Conservatives strong support, it seems that the
proposed tariff revisions merely confirmed their views. The
Conservative candidates, Sandon and Cresswell, made tariff
revision their main electoral theme, denouncing it at meetings of dockers and shippers. At the election, occupations
related to the docking and shipping interest voted overwhelmingly Conservative: pilots voted 54–0 for Sandon and
Cresswell over the Whigs Walmsley and Palmerston; block-
makers, 92–14; coopers, 219–32; ropers and ropemakers,
183–18; sailmakers, 100–31; and shipwrights, 357–67.[21] At
the port of Bristol, where there was an important West
Indian interest, it seems that the Whig proposal to revise the
sugar duty received most attention during the campaign. The
incumbent Whig, F. H. F. Berkeley, was returned with a

protectionist Conservative, P. W. Skinner Miles, in a close election with Miles heading the poll at 4,192 votes and Berkeley edging out the second Conservative, William Fripp, by 3,739 votes to 3,684. Although Berkeley was a brother of the notorious borough magnate, Lord Segrave, it is unlikely that corruption played much of a role at Bristol, where there were more than 10,000 registered voters. Berkeley's victory probably owed much to his specific disavowal of the Whig proposal on sugar. As he declared in an election address: 'I certainly regretted so far to prejudice the principle of the Budget and oppose the government I have generally supported; but I felt that Bristol is deeply interested in the West India Trade—it is the staple of the Port. . . .'[22] Thus, Berkeley was able to reduce somewhat an anticipated Conservative landslide among voters connected with the docking and shipping interests. As the poll book indicates, Berkeley's record among them was better than that of his Whig colleagues at Liverpool. Coopers, for example, gave 55 votes to the two Conservatives, split 11 between Miles and Berkeley, and plumped 25 for Berkeley. Sailmakers voted 8 for the Conservatives, split 2 between Miles and Berkeley, and plumped 3 for Berkeley. Shipwrights voted 56 for the Conservatives, split 11 between Miles and Berkeley, and plumped 25 for Berkeley.[23]

After the borough elections, the county elections were held. The decisive Conservative victory in the counties was directly attributable to the growing unease in the countryside about the Whig policy on the Corn Laws. English farmers especially, an important section of the county electorate, had become increasingly partial to the Conservatives as the party most likely to preserve agricultural protection. Conservative speeches at county hustings during the campaign of 1841 played upon rural fears that the Whigs were contemplating not merely Corn Law revision, but Corn Law abolition. Speeches at nomination day in South Essex typified their approach. The Conservative candidate George Palmer claimed that the Whig government had been influenced 'by the extraordinary infatuation of the political economists, and the delusive theories of the free traders'. It was now the intention of the Whig government, he charged, 'to take away the protection from the agricultural interest'.[24]

The most surprising Conservative victory in the counties came in the West Riding of Yorkshire, where there were several traditional sources of apparently unassailable Whig electoral strength. The dominant influence in the West Riding were the Whigs Earl Fitzwilliam and the Earl of Scarborough. Also, the rural population was less agricultural than many county divisions, for it contained such manufacturing towns as Sheffield, Bradford, and Leeds, the populations of which spilled beyond the boroughs. In addition, the Whig incumbent candidates in 1841, Lords Milton and Morpeth, seemed especially strong. Milton was heir to the Fitzwilliam earldom and Morpeth had served in the Melbourne cabinet as Chief Secretary to Ireland. Yet the Whigs were 'smashed' at the election, as Morpeth put it in a dispirited letter to Lord John Russell.[25] Various reasons may be advanced for their defeat. First, it seems that the local Whig party was not harmonious, and this doubtless had its effect.[26] Second, the unpopularity of the Whig government probably turned Morpeth's cabinet position into a liability. Most important was the adoption of more popular issues by the Conservatives. The Conservative candidates, John Stuart Wortley (the eldest son of Lord Wharncliffe) and Edmund B. Denison, energetically denounced Corn Law reduction. Denison, in his published election address, wrote that the object of the Corn Laws, contrary to Whig claims, was 'to afford employment to our labourers'.[27] At an election meeting in Leeds, Wortley declared it strange that the government, after ignoring the Corn Laws for eleven years, suddenly decided to act—or not so strange, if one realised that it was nothing but 'electioneering clap-trap'.[28] In an interjection unusual for a county campaign, Wortley also condemned the Whigs for the new Poor Law. The Whig government, he wrote, had shown a disposition 'to carry out their theory with a speculative rigour, ill calculated to mitigate whatever there was of harshness in the law and its operation on poorer classes'.[29] It was a direct appeal to the large numbers of non-agricultural county voters in the Riding. Conservative use of issues such as these could well have been decisive in an election in which only 700 out of 50,000 total votes separated the victorious from the defeated candidates. Conservative support seems to have come not only from protectionist farmers but from weavers who occupied small farms near the towns and who opposed the Poor Law. The defeated Whig candidates were well aware of the strength of the issues employed by their opposition. Earl Fitzwilliam blamed the defeat on what he called 'agricultural agitation'.[30] Morpeth thought essentially the same: in his post-election letter to Lord John Russell, he wrote that 'the manufacturing portions of the constituency . . . entirely failed in making any adequate exertion to counteract the known hostility of the agricultural.'[31]

Less easy to assess as a campaign issue was the impact of the anti-Poor Law sentiment. Agitation against the new Poor Law had been building up in the north of England since its passage by the Whigs in 1834. The electoral potential of the anti-Poor Law sentiment was tested at a by-election in Nottingham in April 1841 held several weeks before the general election. The results were not promising for the Whigs. Prior to 1841, Nottingham had long been a Whig borough.[32] Whigs had been returned to both parliamentary seats since 1818. Whigs also dominated municipal politics: among the offices of the corporation in 1839, for example, Whigs held fifty and Conservatives only six. Whig dominance was based upon an extensive popular franchise. Voting rights rested with the 40s freeholders and the freemen of the borough. The largest single occupational group among freemen was the framework-knitters who had

traditionally been anti-Conservative. Declining employment
and the new Poor Law, however, made the borough electorate a fertile recruiting ground for the Conservatives in
the late 1830s. Anti-Poor Law sentiment focused in early
1841 upon the construction of a new Poor House 'of extreme
size'.[33] It was to be 364 ft. long, with a roof reservoir—filled
from the basement with a wheel pump—providing hot and
cold water. There was also to be a water closet for each floor.
These amenities did not allay the alarm among the unemployed working class of Nottingham as the Poor House took
shape: it seemed large enough to house them all. Did the
Whig government intend to force the whole body of the poor
into the new structure, with all its attendant regulations?
The alarm of the poor was only matched by the dismay of
the ratepayers who bore the financial burden of the new
building. At a protest meeting, an opponent of the new
workhouse summed up the opposition when he declared in
favour of the old Poor Law which 'was far more satisfactory
than the present sweeping system of centralisation, with all
its cumbrous machinery—a system which abridged the comforts of the poor, and increased the taxes of the ratepayers'.[34]
During the height of the controversy, one of the sitting
Whig members, Sir Ronald Ferguson, died. The ensuing
by-election pitted a Whig, George Larpent (named 'Larpent
the Sarpent' by his working-class opposition) against the
editor of *The Times*, John Walter. Larpent's platform was
a very progressive one: he supported the ballot and Corn
Law abolition, and was opposed to church rates. Walter
stood simply as an anti-Poor Law candidate and this allowed him, despite his Conservative leanings, to represent
himself as the popular candidate. Although Nottingham
had never been a stranger to corruption, and it seems that
both candidates practised their share at this election, the
issue of the Poor Laws was the deciding factor. Walter won
by slightly more than 200 votes in a total poll of over
3,600: he had won half the votes of the framework knitters.[35]

It was a warning to the Whig government: if Nottingham could fall to the Conservatives, what seat could be called safe?

There was apparently some effort among the Conservatives in their selection of candidates prior to the general election to take advantage of the anti-Poor Law mood of the north. Disraeli, for example, was urged to stand for Leicester because of his known opposition to the new Poor Law.[36] During the campaign, speeches against the new Poor Law were made in quite diverse constituencies including Ipswich, Plymouth, Maidstone, Northampton, the City of London, North Northumberland, and (as noted above) the West Riding of Yorkshire. Conservative candidates usually took the approach that the new Poor Law represented a dangerous centralising tendency by concentrating too much power in the Poor Law Commission. The speech of FitzRoy Kelly at Ipswich was typical. He condemned the Commission as 'those three Inquisitors' and advocated a return of the administration of the Poor Law to local authorities.[37]

Anti-Poor Law sentiment fostered by the Conservatives during the campaign had one surprising result: it contributed to an electoral alliance between Conservatives and Chartists. Opposition to the Whig Poor Law had been one of the important sources of Chartist support during the late 1830s. By making it an election issue, the Conservative platform proved temporarily attractive to the Chartists. Furthermore, Chartist distaste for the Whig ministry had grown in recent years with the attempted suppression of Chartism and the arrest of Chartist leaders. 'Whig tyranny' was a popular election cry among Chartists, one in which Conservatives might gladly join. A further basis of co-operation between Conservatives and Chartists was their common distrust of the growing free-trade movement. To the Chartists, the Whig tariff revision scheme sounded suspiciously close to the free-trade doctrines of the Anti-Corn Law League.

Chartist dislike of the League's free-trade doctrine ran deep. Chartists believed that manufacturers' support of Corn Law repeal was not based upon a generous impulse to provide cheaper bread for workmen, but upon the assumption that cheaper bread prices would allow manufacturers to reduce labour costs by lowering wages. A pamphlet published in 1833 by a well-known Lancashire cotton master, Henry Ashworth, advocated cheap bread on those very grounds.[38] Ashworth wrote with authority. He actively supported the League and served as director and president of the Manchester Chamber of Commerce for several years. He was a close friend of Richard Cobden and brother-in-law of John Bright. It is not surprising that Chartism viewed the League as an instrument of middle-class exploitation, and sought to disrupt League meetings when possible. Chartist disruption of free-trade meetings had begun before the election. They were especially active in the Staffordshire potteries. At Hanley, for example, a local Chartist named Richards, supported by reportedly hundreds of Chartists, spoke against Corn Law abolition at a free-trade meeting.[39] A similar free-trade meeting at Wednesbury was commandeered by a Chartist named Candy.[40] In Leicester, the Chartists set up a rival dais at a free-trade meeting and attacked the proposed Whig tariff reductions as useless to the working man.[41] At York, James Leach, a Chartist lecturer, denounced anti-Corn Law pronouncements: 'the burdens of the people ought first to be removed,' he said 'and then they might talk of free trade'.[42] The Chartist Charles Harris became co-chairman of a Stroud (Gloucestershire) free-trade meeting by the simple expedient of mounting the platform and seating himself next to the delegated chairman. Later in the meeting, Harris spoke of Chartist disappointment with the Whig government, and of the real purpose of Corn Law reduction. 'He would tell the meeting what the gentlemen wanted who called for a repeal of the corn laws—they did not want cheap bread—they wanted cheap labour. . . ."[43] Thus the Chartists were able to counter the Whig electoral cry of 'cheap bread' with their own cry of 'low wages'.

To reach a wider audience from the hustings, the Chartists sponsored a few candidates in their own right. Peter McDouall stood for Northampton, Henry Vincent for Banbury, and George Julian Harney and Lawrence Pitkeithly for the West Riding.[44] The Northampton election provides a clear example of the Chartist–Conservative alliance. Weeks before the election, Northampton Chartists were actively speaking out against the Whig ministry. The Conservative *Northampton Herald* gave them every encouragement. It opened its pages to Chartist letters, and noted with approval Chartist speakers who 'uttered sentiments with which we and every sound Conservative must cordially coincide'. The Chartist campaign was unsuccessful, however. McDouall was last in a field of four and the Conservative, Sir Henry Willoughby, was third. The Chartist–Conservative alliance is evident from the poll book. Of 176 votes cast for McDouall, only 22 split with the Whig candidates while 149 split with Willoughby. Of these 149, it was said that 114 were well-known Conservatives.[45] A more successful Chartist–Conservative alliance was put together at Bradford (Yorks) where the Conservative John Hardy headed the poll. This was the climax to four years of Conservative electioneering among Bradford workingmen, begun with the formation of the Operative Conservative Society. From 1837 to 1840, when technologically displaced handloom weavers provided the bulk of support for Bradford Chartism, the Conservatives continued their efforts to win a working-class constituency, whereas the Whigs confined themselves to organising a local anti-Corn Law campaign. Chartist election overtures to the Conservatives in 1841 assured Hardy of his victory.[46]

Local Chartist leaders were actively collaborating elsewhere with the Conservatives. At an election meeting in

Leeds, a Chartist–Conservative named Parker pledged his support to the banker, William Becket.[47] Becket was returned head of the poll at Leeds, displacing one of the Whig incumbents. Chartist speakers also appeared at the Norwich, Newcastle, Ipswich, Salford, and Tower Hamlets elections. In Gloucester, Henry Vincent, the Chartist lecturer and candidate for Banbury, urged the electorate to vote for the Conservatives. To his audiences, he 'admitted that the Tories were bad enough in all conscience', yet 'they were possessed of more political honestly than their opponents, and have never evinced, even in the palmy days of Castlereagh and spies, such savage cruelty as the Whigs had done in their crusade against the Chartists'.[48]

It is evident that the Chartists, who initiated the alliance, looked upon the Conservatives with hardly more favour than they looked upon the Whigs. It was purely a tactical move. They hoped to defeat the Whigs, and then to force upon them the necessity of wooing Chartist support by political concessions. Feargus O'Connor, editor of the Chartist *Northern Star*, put the case simply: the Chartist must 'use the Tories for the purpose of beating the Whigs'.[49] Or, as one Chartist spokesman declared at Leicester, they made use of the Tories, 'in order to cut, politically, the throats of the Whigs, but when they had procured all that the people required, then they would turn round and cut the throats of the Tories'.[50] The Conservative candidates, not unnaturally, were occasionally reluctant to accept Chartist support. Henry Halford, who shared the hustings with Chartists in his successful candidacy for South Leicestershire, confessed he had felt himself in a 'somewhat strange' position. But, he assured a post-election victory dinner, he had not compromised his Conservative principles by 'any jot or tittle'. He could only explain the Chartist preference for Conservatives as the preference given 'to open and determined enemies, above treacherous and deceitful friends'.[51] Some Conservatives embraced more eagerly the proffered

Chartist support. At the Carlisle (Cumberland) election, Edward Goulburn made a direct appeal for Chartist votes. In a pre-election address, he condemned the Whig prosecutions of the Chartist leaders. On nomination day, he continued to court the Chartists, promising to support a petition for the remission of the sentences of the Chartist leaders and claiming they had not had 'fair play'.[52] Goulburn was unsuccessful but he managed a respectable poll in view of the fact that Conservatives had not contested the seat since 1832.

Such an unlikely combination as a Chartist–Conservative alliance thoroughly alarmed the Whigs. As early as the Nottingham by-election in April 1841, the Whigs thought they saw such a coalition forming. The Whiggish *Bristol Gazette* had written on 22 April of the 'unholy alliance' working in unison at Nottingham. The *Leeds Mercury* had been equally disturbed at the Nottingham result and hoped to discredit the Conservatives by associating them with disreputable characters. 'It would both disgust our readers and the public,' wrote the *Mercury* on 1 May 1841, 'to detail all the arts which the Tory-Chartist-Revolutionary-Socialist-Infidel coalition resort to.' Even in Birmingham, which had an unrivalled reputation for harmony and co-operation between the working-class and middle-class radicals, the Whig majority was so reduced at the general election that the radical Thomas Attwood made a public statement deploring Chartist tactics.[53]

One must not, however, over-emphasise Chartist influence on the election. There was more talk than action. Nor could Chartists exert much direct electoral pressure since most of them were unenfranchised. Furthermore, Chartist leadership was notoriously weak, often divided, and occasionally corrupt. For example, the Norwich Chartist, Dover, apparently accepted a bribe to withdraw the name of a Chartist candidate for the borough. When the Chartist crowd discovered the deception on nomination day, they chased Dover from the public house where he lodged, dis-

armed him (he had drawn a sword against the crowd), and
beat him badly with the shutters ripped from the windows
of the public house. He was in danger of his life when he was
rescued by the borough police.[54] But if Chartist influence
was likely to be decisive at only a few constituencies, it was
another electoral blow that cost the Whigs the election.

The result of the election was no surprise to the country.
The Conservative victory was expected. Nor were there any
surprises in the composition of the new administration. Peel
chose his ministers from the ranks of experienced Conservative leaders, some of whom had served in Peel's first
administration. Among his colleagues, Peel was undoubtedly the most capable. From his earliest day he was, as his
biographer has noted, almost monotonously successful.
After a double first at Oxford, he entered Parliament in
1809 (for the corrupt Irish borough of Cashel). Within
fourteen months he was offered one of the Under-Secretary-
ships of War and Colonies. In 1812, when only twenty-four,
he was appointed Chief Secretary to Ireland. Thereafter, his
rise into the ranks of the Conservative leadership was only
a matter of time. Home Secretary at the age of thirty-four
under Liverpool and then under Wellington, Peel capped his
rise to power by becoming Prime Minister briefly in 1834-5.
Prime Minister again in 1841 at the age of fifty-three and at
the height of his powers, he brought his distinguished public
career to a fitting climax.

Peel's views on government placed him in the ranks of
administrative activists. Strong governments, he thought,
not only achieved more, but were preferred by the governed.
In a letter to a cabinet colleague, he once observed that
'people like a certain degree of obstinacy and presumption
in a minister. They abuse him for dictation and arrogance,
but they like being governed.'[55] On another occasion, when
discussing a problem of Canadian government with his
Secretary of Colonies, he indicated the possibility of govern-
ing by executive means against the wishes of a popular

assembly. 'See what George the third did in 1783–4', he suggested.[56] Peel's tendency toward elitist notions of government was also reflected in his views of parliamentary representation. It was a view that emphasised the independence
of a member from the opinions of his constituents. As Peel
once put it to a correspondent, he acted in Parliament 'not
as a local delegate, having mere local interests and local
feelings to consult, but as the independent member of a great
Legislative Council. . . .'[57] This had echoes of Burkean
sentiment, and, like Burke, Peel seemed to have a strong
distrust of uncontrolled political expressions outside Parliament. Perhaps it was not surprising that a man who
believed in the efficacy of executive government should find
the crosscurrents of public opinion no sure guide to action.
Peel's views of governmental functions were closely allied
with what he considered to be the main aim of government
—the maintenance of public order. His horror of what he
once called 'social distemper'[58] was an important impetus
to his policies. His financial and commercial reforms were
designed to promote public order as much as to relieve the
economic complaints of producers and consumers. His
concern for order may also be seen in his Irish policy.

The personality of Peel seemed to complement perfectly
his views of an efficient and aloof government. Like the
younger Pitt, he found it difficult to unbend before any but
his family and closest associates. The common view of him
was that of Lord Ashley—that he was 'an iceberg'.[59] Peel
refused to suffer fools gladly. He could be impatient with
subordinates. He could be sharp even with his cabinet
colleagues. It was not that he was unkind. He simply exercised to the full his drive for efficiency: small talk was not
his forte. He always felt the press of time in public matters.
But his manner cost him popularity, and his insensitivity to
the good opinions of others was no doubt a factor in his
isolation from the party that brought him to power.

Peel was not insensitive to the social questions of the day.

He was appalled by the revelations of the conditions of the poor during the severe winter of 1841–2. He made personal contributions on two occasions to the charities of the city of Paisley. He expressed sympathy for the demands of the striking colliers during the Plug Plot of 1842. He thought their working conditions and wage reductions justified complaint and that colliery owners' profits were high enough for them to 'deal much more liberally with their workmen than they do'.[60] But Peel did not translate what humanitarian impulses he may have had into a passion for reform. His undoubted sympathy with the plight of the working man did not outweigh his caution in advocating meliorative legislation. This was a caution upheld by his cabinet. Their tendency was to make the existing laws more efficient rather than to extend the active role of the state in social and economic matters. Thus, the Peel ministry resisted the two foremost reformist influences of the time: Benthamism and organised philanthropy. Peel was doubtful whether Parliament could ease economic and social inequities by direct legislative action. He was especially fearful that the tradition of cheap and limited government would be imperilled by an extension of government authority. Furthermore, an overactive government might dampen the enthusiasm of capital in promoting growth. As the son of a wealthy cotton manufacturer, Peel retained a firm sympathy with the competitive entrepreneurial ideal. Yet he obviously recognised the dangers of unchecked growth and its disastrous social consequences. For Peel, then, the role of government was to serve as a balance between the broad categories of producers and consumers. The interests of both had to be protected: economic grievances of working men had to be met as far as possible without impeding the expansion of the economy.

Peel saw tariff reform as the ideal instrument to achieve the delicate balance he sought. By reducing tariff duties on important articles of consumption, such as grain and meat,

gland, Graham rejected it as a provocative act and thought it would be 'the signal of insurrection in the South'.[68] Furthermore, Wellington's relations with Peel were occasionally ruffled. Their lack of warmth for one another, dating from the time when Peel had served as Home Secretary under Wellington from 1828 to 1830, was not eased by Peel's stiffness and Wellington's advancing years and deafness, which exacerbated small misunderstandings. Tensions between the two, however, were inevitably smoothed over, primarily by Wellington's ability to see himself as entirely in agreement with Peel after all. Similar to Wellington in pugnacity of spirit was Edward Law, Lord Ellenborough, who served in the cabinet only briefly as President of the Board of Control before his appointment in late 1841 as Governor-General of India. Once in India and far removed from the restraints of his cabinet colleagues, Ellenborough's deeply felt imperial sentiments found full expression in the addition of Scinde to the Indian Empire, much to Peel's displeasure.

Another uneasy colleague in the cabinet was the Secretary for War and Colonies, Lord Stanley. Stanley, like Graham, had begun his political life as a Whig. His evolution as a Conservative did not cease with the middle ground of Graham, however. He broke with Peel's commercial policy in 1845 over the Corn Laws, to become head of the protectionist faction and anti-Peelite. Even before then, however, he had not been happy in the cabinet: he felt too restricted by the minutiae of finance and commerce which his office required. At his own request in 1844, he was raised to the House of Lords, where he had a freer play upon the whole of public policy.

Further sources of division in the cabinet were Sir Edward Knatchbull and the Duke of Buckingham. They were added to the cabinet purely for political reasons because they represented the agricultural protectionist right wing of the party. The protectionists had been instrumental in returning Conservative candidates in the counties during the general election, and some official recognition of them was necessary. Peel was under no illusion as to their contribution to the government. He confided to Wellington that he thought Buckingham's only concern was 'his private interest' and that he would support the government only so far as that was satisfied.[69] Buckingham was given the Privy Seal and Knatchbull made Paymaster General. Neither man finished his term of office. Buckingham resigned early in 1842 over the terms of the budget and was replaced by the Duke of Buccleuch. Knatchbull, never comfortable in the cabinet, hung on until February 1845, to be replaced by W. B. Baring, the son of Lord Ashburton.

Four other cabinet members played subordinate roles. Peel felt obliged to them for their support in the abortive ministry of 1834–5. They were the Earl of Haddington at the Admiralty; Sir Henry Hardinge, Secretary at War; Lord Lyndhurst, Lord Chancellor (a position he had twice filled before); and Lord Wharncliffe, Lord President of the Council. More important to the cabinet was the Chancellor of the Exchequer, Henry Goulburn. To have served as Chancellor of the Exchequer to Peel must have taken a man with great qualities of self-effacement. Indeed, Goulburn seems most often to have served as a sounding-board for Peel's fiscal views, and as the administration wore on, his role developed into one more resembling that of a civil servant than a cabinet minister.[70] Somewhat puzzling was the role of Frederick John Robinson, the first Earl of Ripon, who served as President of the Board of Trade until 1843 and thereafter as President of the Board of Control. Ripon, who had the distinction of serving as prime minister for the shortest length of time in British history—three inglorious months in 1827—was scarcely a tower of strength. He was plagued by ill-health and seemed feckless and indecisive in administration. If Ellenborough is to be believed, Peel himself held a low opinion of Ripon's tenure at the Board of Control and had been obliged to do much of

Ripon's work for him.[71] Even Ripon's recent biographer can find little to praise in him beyond his amiability and his character.[72] Ripon did bring to the cabinet a long acquaintance with the administrative machinery of trade and economics, having served with the Board of Trade as early as 1812. More important to Peel was his experience and inclination that had made him a fiscal liberal in the Peelite mould. Soon after the new government was formed, Ripon sent to Peel a series of letters which urged the revision of Britain's commercial policy. He suggested reduction of duties upon corn, sugar, timber and coffee, and the possibility of trade treaties with other nations. Peel advised Ripon to exercise caution with his plan, warning that 'the agricultural mind would be very sensitive' to any relaxation of the Corn Laws.[73] Although Peel thought Ripon might be moving too fast in the early days of the new administration, Ripon's support for Peel's commercial policy was very welcome in later days.

Serving in the government at first as Vice-President of the Board of Trade under Ripon was W. E. Gladstone, at the beginning of his public career that was to span the remainder of the century. Gladstone had previously served in the brief Peel ministry of 1834–5 as an Under-Secretary to the Treasury, and since then had continued to impress his colleagues by his powers of application and sense of duty. When Ripon left the Board of Trade to take the Board of Control, Gladstone took his place with a seat in the cabinet. In late 1845, he became Colonial Secretary when Stanley resigned over the Corn Laws. His inclinations toward a liberal commercial policy seconded those of Peel and Ripon. Gladstone's weaknesses were also only too evident, but they were more exasperating than crippling to the government. His overdeveloped sense of scruple led him to an unnecessary resignation from the cabinet in 1845. He seemed unable to realise, as a friend put it, that a politician needed a strong, rather than a tender conscience.[74] Gladstone's subtleties of mind extended—to the annoyance of his colleagues and the confusion of the House of Commons—to his memoranda and speeches. His syntactical obscurities were an impediment to business and once drove Peel to complain that Gladstone's 'very hard English' gave him a 'head ache'.[75] But his sense of duty and mastery of detail made up for all.

Foreign policy as conducted by the Peel administration is generally held to be a subject of only minimal interest. Standard works on British foreign policy scarcely find room for Peel's Foreign Secretary, Lord Aberdeen, sandwiched as he was between the terms of office of the more flamboyant Palmerston. Contrasted with Palmerston, Aberdeen has seemed weak, incompetent, and even indolent in the pursuit of foreign policy.[76] It is true that Aberdeen, occasionally bold in the conception of his diplomatic schemes, was less so in the execution of them. He was much more likely than Palmerston to defer to the opinion of his colleagues. His withdrawn, pessimistic, and slightly hypochondriacal nature may account for his lapses of energy. Or he may have lacked the necessary ambition and ruthlessness. Yet his finer qualities were also evident. He was an experienced diplomat. When a young man, he had gone to Vienna in 1813 with Castlereagh. He had served as Foreign Secretary in the Wellington ministry of 1828–30, and as Colonial Secretary in Peel's short ministry of 1834–5. He was less presumptuous, perhaps more humane than Palmerston; and he was unswerving in his dedication to peace in Europe, above all with France. His preference for conciliation rather than confrontation was to have fortunate consequences, for events abroad between 1841 and 1846 dictated an uneasy time for the administration. French and American expansionist policies challenged established British supremacy at many points. Inherited wars in China and India, which altered the shape of the empire, were further sources of strain. Peel's administration had fully as much to occupy its attention in foreign as in domestic affairs, and in that administration Aberdeen played a not insignificant part.

The construction of Peel's cabinet and its performance during its first two years gave an appearance of awesome inpregnability. The strength of the cabinet was twofold. First, it had experienced men whose administrative talents were first-rate. Peel, Graham, Gladstone, and Goulburn were all notably efficient ministers. This was a welcome change from the more lackadaisical methods of Melbourne and Russell. Second, in spite of its eventual fissiparous tendency, the cabinet acted initially as a cohesive unit under Peel. As Ripon had rightly observed to Graham, the key to success of the new government would be 'undeviating confidence to the *leader*'.[77] But if the strength of the cabinet was Peel, so was its weakness. Convinced of his own rectitude, Peel did not find a colleague sufficiently strong in the cabinet to challenge his views, and at times he became unapproachably rigid. Peel's maintenance of an eighteenth-century executive prerogative was an anachronism within a House of Commons that was increasingly aware of its duty to opinion in the country at large. In short, Peel's ministry was strong administratively, but weak politically.

The political weakness of the ministry was long obscured by the weakness of its parliamentary opposition. There was a noticeable apathy in the ranks of the Whigs after the election—perhaps natural for a party unaccustomed to the role of opposition after so many years in power. One would expect a pause while forces re-grouped. Personal considerations may also have contributed to Whig inactivity: Melbourne was deteriorating, and Lord John Russell had a new wife, whom he married during the general election. But the main reason for Whig ineffectiveness was that Peel's initiatives kept the Whigs off-balance. Much of the Conservative programme offered battlegrounds uncongenial to the Whigs, who lacked the financial expertise of the Conservative leadership. Unable to oppose Conservative legislative initiatives effectively, the Whigs were reduced to a hunt for issues: they did not often find them. Ireland provided one rare opportunity in 1844 and the Corn Laws another in late 1845. It was clear, however, that the Whigs lacked a policy. The Irish under O'Connell provided some opposition to the ministry, but their numbers and influence in Parliament had declined during the general election. O'Connell himself, though still capable of rousing the Irish countryside, was ageing and less forceful than in the days of Catholic Emancipation. Indeed, the Irish threatened to be more of a problem to the Whigs than to the Conservatives. The Whigs recognised that it was electorally disadvantageous to continue to act with O'Connell, especially during the repeal agitation. Yet an open break with the Irish radical leader could also be damaging. In the end, it was Peel who brought down his own ministry as his liberalised Irish and commercial policies alienated the rural, Protestant, protectionist wing of the Conservative party. Only when the Conservative party was broken in the fatal days of 1846 did the opposition find the strength to force Peel's resignation.

2 DOMESTIC POLICY: FINANCIAL AND SOCIAL

The early promise of the new ministry was best realised in certain of its domestic policies, of which financial reform was the most important. As Professor Gash has observed, what parliamentary reform had been to Lord Grey's ministry in 1830, financial reform was to Peel's in 1841.[1] Through the instrument of the budget, Peel initiated two major programmes, tariff reform and the first peace-time income tax in Britain's history. The programmes were complementary: with the revenue generated by the income tax, it would be possible to enact a considerable reduction of tariff duties. Reduced import duties would not only encourage trade but provide cheaper goods for British consumers as well. As corollaries to its budgetary programmes, the ministry reduced the interest on the consolidated funds, and reformed the business practices of banks and corporations. These extensive measures of governmental intervention in the private sector of the economy contributed significantly to the financial stability of the country.

Before the ministry's financial policy was finally determined, some initial cabinet objections had to be overcome. An income tax was never popular: Parliament's removal of the previous war-time income tax was celebrated in 1816 by a gleeful burning of the tax records. Stanley thought an income tax was an unwise measure even though the ministry was 'driven to attempt it'; and Graham warned that 'the Republicans' would agitate for a graduated tax as soon as the issue was brought forward.[2] On the other hand, the Chancellor of the Exchequer, Goulburn, believed that an income tax would be more acceptable because of the 'immense increase' of taxable income since 1815.[3] After a campaign of gentle persuasion, Peel convinced his more reluctant colleagues of the necessity of an income tax.

Tariff reform was even more dangerous politically than the income tax, for it echoed one of the unsuccessful election slogans of the previous Whig administration. Peel's ministry had been returned with the implicit understanding—at least in the minds of the gentry and farmers—that the Corn Laws would remain inviolate. Was Peel willing to make an exception to tariff reform in the case of corn? The answer was no. Since corn was, along with timber, sugar, and coffee, one of the most highly valued imports, it would be impossible for Peel to exclude it. Peel maintained that tariff reform did not mean an abandonment of protection, but he advocated what he called fair, rather than excessive, protection. His cabinet could agree with this moderate position, although they did so from different vantage-points. Ripon believed that the domestic grower of wheat ought to be satisfied with less than he was guaranteed under the existing Corn Law. He justified a relaxation of the Corn Law on the grounds that it was 'questionable' whether the domestic grower could produce enough for an increasing population.[4] Grain imports would eventually become necessary. Ripon further believed that the colonies, especially Canada, ought to be encouraged to fill the projected need of grain imports. Contrary to Ripon, Graham believed that domestic agricultural production could keep pace with population growth through extensive improvements. An active improver himself, Graham had brought his own estate at Netherby to a high pitch of efficiency through drainage, enclosure, and the careful selection of tenants. Comparable improvements throughout the kingdom would make British agriculture competitive with foreign agricultural imports, rendering a high Corn Law unnecessary. Therefore, he agreed with Ripon that 50s-60s per quarter of wheat was an adequate price to the domestic grower. This represented a change in Graham's opinion. When he had helped draw up the Report of the Agriculture Committee of 1833, he had held that Britain's productive capacity would be unable to match its population growth. As Graham wrote to Peel, his own change of mind indicated how unwise it was 'to dogmatise in matters of this highly speculative character!'[5]

The only cabinet member who remained unconverted to tariff reform was the protectionist Duke of Buckingham: he resigned in January 1842, to be replaced by the Duke of Buccleuch. Buckingham was not a great loss to the cabinet, but he had some standing among the protectionist back-benchers. His resignation apparently decided the cabinet to make Corn Law revision an issue separate from general tariff reform and to introduce it at the beginning of the 1842 session.[6] Thus a matter of delicacy for the party could be settled early.

Peel opened the session of 1842 with the proposed new Corn Law. Rejecting the Whig policy of a fixed duty on corn as too rigid, Peel declared his administration to be in favour of the existing sliding scale of duties which varied inversely with the price of corn in the domestic market. Although the sliding scale was retained, the duties dependent on that scale were reduced considerably. For example, under the old Corn Law, when the domestic price of wheat was between 59s and 60s, foreign wheat might enter only at a duty of 27s 8d per quarter. The proposed new bill would reduce that duty to 13s. Comparable reductions were made down the scale. Peel admitted that the proposed bill would mean 'a very considerable decrease of the protection' previously given to the home grower.[7] But he reminded his agricultural supporters that it was necessary to protect the interests of consumers as well as those of the producers.

There was some opposition, as anticipated, from the

Whigs and from the noisy knot of free traders. The Whig opposition was mild, however. Lord John Russell focused his attention on the principle of the sliding scale, but his motion in favour of a fixed duty as a substitute was easily defeated. For the free traders, Cobden denounced the measure 'as an insult to the suffering people'[8] and Villiers moved his annual motion favouring free trade. After several nights of debate, Villiers' motion lost by a vote of 393-90, with many of the Whigs voting against it. The Whig vote against Villiers demonstrated that their moderate protectionism was not far removed from the policy of the Conservative leadership. The real difference between Peel and the Whigs lay in the means by which each would secure that policy—the Whigs favouring the fixed duty, and Peel the sliding scale. The Whigs were not yet free traders. A half-expected protectionist rebellion never developed. Apart from an amendment—subsequently withdrawn—by R. A. Christopher (Lincolnshire North) to raise duties a few shillings at the lower end of the scale, and a few grumbling speeches by W. S. Blackstone (Wallingford), the Conservative agricultural backbenchers said little.

On 11 March 1842, Peel introduced the income tax. Deploring the 'wretched expedient of continued loans'[9] to meet the budgetary needs of the state, Peel declared the necessity of unusual measures. So large were the anticipated deficits projected for the following year (incurred, it was intimated, by faulty Whig finance) that there was an immediate need for substantial revenues. The Prime Minister then appealed to the 'possessors of property' for their aid in ending the long history of budget deficits: only their help would stem 'the annual growth of this mighty evil'.[10] The proposed tax, Peel assured the House, would not be permanent. It would be retained only until the emergency had passed. Three years was the intended limitation. Furthermore, the proposed tax was light: only 7*d* in the pound (or 3 percent) for annual incomes above £150. Incomes below

£150 would be exempted. To make it more palatable to the landed interest, Peel declared that the tax charged to farmers would be on a lower assessment of their rents than the previous wartime tax. The earlier tax had estimated profits for English farmers at 75 percent of their rentals. The new tax would estimate profits at only 50 percent of rentals. Scots farmers had previously been assessed at 50 percent of rentals; the new tax lowered it to 33.3 percent. The new tax would not apply to Ireland. Instead, a duty of 1s per gallon on spirits manufactured in Ireland would be levied, and Irish stamp duties would be increased.

By appealing to a sense of duty among his supporters, and representing the income tax as a temporary measure, Peel greatly lessened what reluctance there may have been among the wealthy to tax themselves. The Whig opposition was also surprisingly light. The cabinet decision to introduce the income tax had been a closely kept secret and its announcement seems to have caught the Whigs off guard. In the weeks of debate, there were a few references on the Whig side to the 'inquisitorial nature' of an income tax, and a comparison to the *taille* and the *gabelle*, but such criticisms were not sustained. There was even an admission—to a chorus of 'hear! hear!' from the Treasury Bench—from the Liberal member for Salford, Joseph Brotherton, that opposition in his own constituency was less than he had expected.[11] The royal assent to the tax proposal was received in late June.

By early May 1842, with the corn law passed and the tax proposal well under way, Peel was ready to bring forward the details of the remainder of the tariff revision scheme. In a comprehensive speech on 10 May 1842, he declared his two main objectives: the simplification of the existing tariff law, and the reduction of the cost of living for the domestic consumer. To the nearly 1,200 dutiable articles, the ministry applied the following principles: removal of prohibitory duties; reduction of duties on raw materials to very low levels, not exceeding 5 percent; reduction of duties on partially manufactured articles, not exceeding 12 percent; reduction of duties on wholly manufactured articles, not exceeding 20 percent; and reduction of duties on colonial produce. The application of these principles reduced duties on some 750 articles.

Debate on individual clauses of the proposed tariff began in late May. Generally speaking, the Whig opposition was scattered and ineffective. The fact that the Whig budget of 1841 had included tariff reduction left them little room for political manoeuvring. The most serious opposition to tariff revision arose from the ranks of nominal administration supporters, the Conservative back-benchers who represented agricultural constituencies. They disliked the proposed reduction of duties on cattle and meat imports. Previously, imports of live cattle and meat were prohibited. The new tariff imposed only a small duty of 15s per head of live cattle (or 7s 6d if from British possessions), and 8s per cwt on salted beef (or 2s from British possessions). Envisioning a flood of cattle and meat from the Continent, farmers exerted pressure on their members in Parliament to request an increase in the ministry's proposed schedule of duties. On 23 May, William Miles (East Somerset) moved an amendment requiring duty on live cattle to be imposed by weight rather than by head. If the amendment were successful, the protectionists hoped to impose a high enough duty per pound to maintain protection. Peel strongly opposed the amendment. He informed the House that he had recently spoken to a deputation of agriculturists who requested a restoration of protective duties. 'To their demand I could not, I cannot accede,' Peel stated. 'I have a deep impression, a firm conviction,' he continued, 'that population is increasing more rapidly than the supply of provision in this country, and that no advantage can be derived by the agriculturists from keeping up higher duties than I propose.'[12] Although the Miles amendment had no chance of success, it mustered as many as 113 votes, 85 of whom were Peel's usual supporters, against the ministry's 382.[13] The vote was the final hurdle for the ministry. Tariff revision received the royal assent on 9 July 1842.

The budget debate in the following year was not protracted; the ministry offered nothing new and was content to allow tariff reduction to work its way. There was, however, ministerial embarrassment because fiscal expectations of the 1842 budget were unrealised. As Goulburn reported to the House of Commons, the continuing industrial depression reduced revenue, forcing upon the ministry a deficit of slightly more than £3 million. Peel effectively disarmed criticism by admitting that he had been wrong in his calculations. He made a point of defending the income tax, noting that the deficit would have been worse without it. The House was inclined to accept his defence.

One important measure in 1843 that extended the policy set down the previous year was the Canadian Corn Bill introduced by Stanley in May. Stanley proposed to admit Canadian corn at a nominal duty of 1s a quarter. It was, he declared, a matter of imperial preference, not a question of freer trade. But protectionist backbenchers did not see it that way. Gilbert Heathcote (Rutland) objected to any further change in the Corn Laws. There was already, he declared, 'a very sore and wounded feeling among the agriculturists' because of the changes of the previous session.[14] William Ormsby Gore (North Salop) declared his stand against 'any further innovation' in the Corn Laws.[15] Although three protectionist amendments offered against the bill were easily defeated, they indicated a growing unease among protectionists with Peel's tariff policy.

Budget news for the government was better in 1844. As Goulburn reported in April of that year, excise estimates had proved quite accurate—only £100,000 short of the estimated £13 million. Customs revenues were even more heartening: they had exceeded expectations by more than £2 million. Much of this came from the new duties on corn, wine, sugar, and tea imports. The increase in tea and sugar imports was especially gratifying to the government, Goulburn reported, for it gave 'satisfactory indications of the revived power of consumption on the part of the labouring population of the country'.[16] The ministry pushed ahead with its policy of reducing duties in its budget for 1844. There were excise reductions on flint glass and vinegar; customs reductions included coffee and currants. In justifying a reduction of currant duties from 22s to 15s per cwt, Goulburn declared that currants 'entered largely into the consumption of the lower and working orders of society, and afford them a luxury which is most agreeable to them. . . .'[17] More important to the consumer was the announcement that the ministry intended to reduce duties on sugar imports. Since sugar duties were debated as an issue separate from the budget, they will be discussed below.

By 1845 it was clear that the combination of a small income tax and tariff reduction had proved workable. In the budget debates of 1845, the ministry revealed that the previous year's budget had yielded a surplus of over £5 million. Therefore Peel (who, rather than Goulburn, presented the budget in 1845) abolished customs duties on 430 dutiable goods, the most important of which was raw cotton. There was another substantial reduction of sugar duties. Some excise duties were abolished, including those on glass. The loss to the revenue was estimated at £3.3 million. To offset this, Peel extended the income tax for another three years.

The Whigs offered little opposition to the budget—even to the proposed continuation of the income tax. As Peel wrote to the queen, the Whigs somewhat inconsistently denounced the tax, yet declared that they would vote for its continuance.[18] Once again, the Conservative backbenchers were the most active opponents of the ministry's budget. They complained, in the words of George Bankes (Dorset), that the budget 'gave everything to the manufacturing and commercial interest, and did nothing for the agricultural'.[19] In a time of agricultural depression, said Sir John Tyrell (Essex North), the agriculturists 'had a fair claim to some expression of commiseration' from the ministry.[20] On 10 March, William Miles (East Somerset) moved that farmers be allowed an appeal on assessment of rent for taxing purposes. This was defeated, however, as was a motion moved a week later, again by Miles, that in any reduction of taxes by the ministry, 'due regard' be given to the relief of the agricultural interest. Publicly the ministry remained impassive during the agricultural attacks. Graham declared that agricultural distress was not widespread, and that there had been a general improvement in the countryside. Peel also discounted the extent of an agricultural depression; he rebuked his rebellious backbenchers and announced his intention 'to pursue the course we have hitherto taken, without yielding. . . ."[21] Privately, the cabinet was more worried. In a letter to the Conservative publicist, John Wilson Croker, Graham wrote that the existence of the government was endangered by the ill-humour of the protectionist country gentry.[22] Although Graham had a tendency to exaggerate the darker side of political life, there is little doubt that the Conservative backbenchers had, by early 1845, a solid core of grievances against their own party leadership.

Excluded from our discussion thus far has been the ministry's policy on sugar. It had always been a special case. Sugar was the leading article of what Gladstone once called 'the luxuries of the labouring classes'—the others being molasses, tea, tobacco, malt, spirits of all kinds, coffee, and cocoa. Sugar had a notoriously high price-elasticity of demand: when its price went up, demand went down in a direct ratio. The importance of sugar to domestic consumers was reflected in the fact that approximately one-third of the total return from the customs was sugar duties, making it the most valuable single item of dutiable imports. Peel's policy of reducing consumer prices would logically lead him to find new sugar suppliers, especially since the traditional source of supply, the British West Indies, was failing. Opportunities for this were severely limited, however, for the ministry was pledged to exclude all slave-grown sugar. Java and the Philippines were possible sources of free sugar, but even here there were difficulties, for in Java, at least, slavery existed to some degree. The dangers of injecting a moral issue into commercial affairs were well recognised by some of the cabinet. Goulburn thought that commercial treaties ought to be concerned with goods 'independent of the mode of their production'.[23] Stanley agreed. But Gladstone, who felt most strongly about the slavery issue, was firm on the matter. Peel, too, believed that the slavery issue ought to count. In any case, it would have been difficult to reverse a policy that had been set at the general election in 1841 when the Conservatives had taken up the anti-slavery cry against the Whigs.

In the face of such difficulties, the cabinet decided not to touch sugar during the sessions of 1842 and 1843 and to maintain the existing duties, which amounted to 25s 3d per cwt on British colonial sugar and 63s on foreign. The government justified its inaction by claiming the revenue as necessary in the case of colonial sugar, and advancing the anti-slavery argument in the case of foreign sugar. However, inaction on sugar gave the opposition a convenient issue. By portraying themselves as the champions of the consumer, the opposition could turn Peel's own policy against him. In the session of 1842, Lord John Russell claimed 'that nothing in the whole range of the customs duties that were proposed to be reduced would more benefit the people of this country' than a reduction of the sugar duties.[24] This was echoed by others. In the session of 1843, Joseph Brotherton (Salford) protested against the administration's policy of 'depriving the poor of their comforts'. The free trader, C. P. Villiers (Wolverhampton), claimed that the anti-slavery argument was merely a pretext on the part of the administration to maintain a protectionist system.[25]

Increasing parliamentary criticism and rising sugar prices forced the ministry to propose reductions on sugar duties in the budget of 1844. The proposed duties were 34s a cwt for foreign sugar and 24s for colonial (plus the customary 5 percent). This was a reduction by half in foreign sugar duties, although a preferential colonial duty still remained. Opposition speeches focused on the differential between colonial and foreign sugar, suggesting that colonial duties should be either abolished or made nominal. The proposal seemed a blatant favouring of the West India interest. If so, the West Indians did not recognise it: they disliked the declining differential between colonial and foreign sugars as proposed by the bill. On 14 June 1844, Philip Miles (Bristol), who had been a protectionist member of Parliament since 1837 and was a strong West Indian spokesman, moved to retain the proposed foreign duty of 34s, but to reduce the colonial duty from 24s to 20s. It was an ingenious proposal. It offered a higher protection to colonial sugar by increasing the duty differential between foreign and colonial sugar. Yet it also made imported sugar even cheaper than the ministry's proposal. Thus the free traders and the colonists could support the bill. More importantly, Miles hoped to attract the support of the agriculturists to his amendment. He stressed the principle of protection as a bond between the colonists and the agriculturists. Miles also warned the agriculturists that if the colonists were abandoned over sugar, the agriculturists in turn might be abandoned over corn. His main objective was obviously to rally protectionists of every stripe against the ministry. It was a remarkably candid appeal to interest, and it worked. The ministry's motion lost by twenty votes. Miles' floor-led protectionist rebellion placed the ministry in an awkward position. Peel was angered to the point of resignation, but cooler heads prevailed and within a few days Miles' motion was rescinded. The Miles affair was a clear warning to the ministry. The principle of protection, which Peel's policies had steadily eroded since 1841, could occasionally attract enough support to place the ministry in jeopardy. As one of the protectionists who voted against Peel put it, 'while we support a Minister, we must also support a principle'.[26]

Sugar continued to plague the ministry in the session of 1845. Graham complained that 'sugar sticks to our fingers and we cannot wash our hands of it'.[27] The ministry's tariff reforms in that session lowered sugar duties from 24s a cwt to 14s on colonial and from 34s to 23s 4d on foreign free sugar. The opposition demanded not only lower duties but also a vigorous policy to encourage an expanded sugar supply. To prohibit slave-grown sugar was, in Lord John's opinion, 'illusory'. Lord John also pointed out the inconsistency of a policy that prohibited foreign slave sugar and yet admitted cotton from the slave-owning southern United States.[28] Macaulay, whose abolitionist credentials were impeccable, took the point further. Although slavery abroad was deplorable, he said, the first obligation the ministry had was to its own countrymen. And the fact was that new supplies of sugar could contribute significantly to the well-being of the domestic labourer.[29] Supporting the ministry, Gladstone defended the sugar policy on moral grounds, although he did admit that the distinction between slave and free sugar could not always 'be drawn with uniform and absolute precision. . . .'[30] Peel and Graham argued from a different standpoint. Graham frankly admitted that some 'consideration' was due to the West Indian interest. Peel also pleaded for fairness to colonial growers: if the cheaper slave-grown sugar were admitted, it would so 'disable' the colonists as to 'incapacitate them from supporting their present burdens. . . .'[31] With the ministry's agricultural supporters remaining firm this time, the Whig attack was blunted and the ministry passed its reductions as introduced.

Thus Peel succeeded in establishing the budget as the most effective instrument of his ministry's domestic policy. Much of the success was due directly to Peel: few could match his mastery of financial detail, or his imagination in making fresh approaches to perplexing problems. A testament to his financial talents was the later success of Gladstone, his most apt pupil. In spite of the undoubtedly favourable impression made on Parliament and the country at large by Peel's budgets, there remained the insistent and nagging backbench opposition to Peel's reduction of agricultural protection. Peel's unrivalled financial talents were never translated to the political arts and he was unwilling to take the time to smooth over his differences with the protectionists. It was a mistake for which he paid dearly in 1846.

Three further measures complemented the ministry's budgetary policy: the reduction of the National Debt, the Joint Stock Companies Regulation Act, and the Bank Charter Act. All were passed in 1844. Early in the session of 1844, Goulburn opened an attack on the National Debt by proposing the reduction of 3½ percent consols to 3¼. The immediate gain to the revenue would be £625,000 annually. There was no parliamentary opposition to the scheme, and very little among stockholders. Upon a conversion of £250 million of stock, only £247,115 was paid off to 'dissentients' (as Goulburn called them). It was a very smooth operation and contributed to the government's reputation as one which shaped the Victorian budgetary tradition of reducing the National Debt and extending free trade.[32]

A similarly easy passage was accorded the Joint Stock Companies Registration and Regulation Act of 1844, the necessity for which was widely recognised. Since the repeal of the Bubble Act in 1825, joint stock companies were freed from the stringent government regulations which had inhibited their growth for more than a century. Thus began a scale of investment hitherto unknown as promoters pressed upon clients projects of every sort, ranging from docks and railways to gas and water companies.[33] There were inevitable reactions, however. Highly touted companies collapsed and the failure of unrealised schemes brought ruin to many. Too often, companies were poorly constructed or (in Gladstone's words) 'unwisely conceived'. Of special concern was the emergence of the new 'bubble companies'. These fraudulent companies were becoming a serious problem as increasing numbers of gullible investors were lured by misleading prospectuses into financial disaster. To protect the public from unscrupulous or unwise company directors, Gladstone, as President of the Board of Trade, brought forward in July 1844 the administration's plan for regulating joint stock companies. It established a public office—the Registrar of Companies—to which anyone could go 'to know the real history of these companies'.[34] All partnerships with more than twenty-five members and freely transferable shares were required to register: and company directors had to present a fully audited balance sheet periodically to the Registrar. These and other regulatory provisions helped protect the public against speculative excesses and created a more responsible climate for company development. It marked, as one historian has observed, 'an epoch in the history of English company law'.[35]

Perhaps the best-known financial act of the session was the Bank Charter Act of 1844. In legislating on the functions of the Bank of England, the ministry exercised an option provided in an 1833 Act, which had renewed the privileges of the Bank for twenty-one years with a proviso that the government might reconsider the subject in ten years. Obvious deficiencies in banking practice in recent years, especially with regard to note issue, motivated the ministry to reconsider. Theoretically the Act of 1819 (also known as Peel's Act, for his role in its passage), which had put the currency back on the gold standard after the suspension of cash payments in 1797, ensured adequate bullion to cover note issue. But between 1826 and 1844 over-issue by provincial banks had caused the failure of 100 banks, or approximately a quarter of all private or joint-stock banks entitled to issue their own notes.[36] Even the Bank of England's bullion reserves had occasionally been too low to support convertibility easily. In 1839, there had been public humiliation when it was learned that the Bank had to borrow £2 million from the Bank of France through the Baring Brothers in order to maintain the convertibility of its bank notes. Throughout 1840 and 1841, the reserve was usually less than £5 million, and often less than £4 million.[37] The banking inquiries of 1826, 1832, 1836–8 and 1840–1 gave evidence of parliamentary concern.

Even these obvious difficulties of an unregulated note issue did not convince everyone of the need for change. The so-called banking school believed that the volume of currency issued should be left to the discretion of bankers. They opposed any attempt on the part of government to restrict the quantity of paper money issued. By the 1840s, however, advocates of a second point of view, the currency school, were gaining ground. They believed that the function of a bank was less the transaction of business than the maintenance of a sufficient reserve on behalf of the nation to enable it to meet its liabilities with other countries. As a corollary, the currency advocates believed that note issue ought to be more closely tied to bullion reserves than the banking adherents were willing to allow.

Peel was a convinced currency man, emphasising the larger economic responsibility of banks. He was careful to draw a distinction between the conduct of ordinary banking business and the issuing of notes: his concern was with the latter. To that end, he proposed two major reforms within the Bank Charter Act. The first concerned the Bank of England. The Bank was divided into a banking department and a note-issuing department. After August 1844, the Bank could not issue notes except when tied to bullion. The second reform concerned country banks. The right of issuing notes would be restricted to those country banks that possessed the privilege as of 1844. Thus, the Act recognised 207 private banks and 72 joint-stock banks with note-issuing power. The amount of note issue of each country bank was not to exceed the average issue of the twelve weeks prior to 27 April 1844.

Peel's ultimate aim was to reduce the rights of issue of the country banks and concentrate them within the Bank of England. He could not move too quickly in that direction, however, for to do so might jeopardise the whole measure. There were many supporters of country banks in the House of Commons who had to be coaxed into the view of seeing local banks as part of a wider, national banking scheme. The measure of Peel's success may be seen in the gradual decline of country banks over subsequent decades until by 1901 there were only 33 private banks and 27 joint-stock banks. By 1918, with the emergence of the Big Five joint-stock banks, there were few survivors of the country banking era, although the last country notes did not disappear until 1921.

In contrast to the ministry's financial policy, its social policy—affecting the poor, the insane, factory and other workers, and a newly created down-trodden class, railway passengers—was essentially cautious. The ministry's social legislation sought to tidy up the loose administrative ends of existing programmes rather than to advance new ones. Had it not been for the initiatives of Lord Ashley, the record of social legislation during Peel's administration would probably have been less than it was. In spite of its fundamentally cautious approach, the ministry encountered far more opposition to its social legislation than to its financial legislation. This opposition was due partly to the controversial nature of the issues involved, and partly to the growing disenchantment of some Conservative backbenchers with their leadership.

The ministry's Poor Law policy exemplified its cautious approach. There was general agreement in the cabinet that the new Poor Law was a success. Since 1834, it had had the desired effect of implementing a more efficient system of poor relief and lowering the poor rates. But the Law was unpopular in the countryside. As we have seen, it was an election issue in 1841. Consequently, some Conservative back-benchers returned at the election were pledged to a revision of the Poor Law. In this aim, they were joined by a group of like-minded radicals.

The most prominent of the anti-Poor Law MPs was William Busfield Ferrand, returned for Knaresborough in 1841. Although a Conservative country squire, Ferrand described himself as 'the advocate of the cause of the working classes of the North of England. . . .'[38] He was also a convinced factory reformer, having been dramatically converted to the cause one winter's day in 1833 when he discovered a comatose factory child buried in a snowdrift near his estate at Bingley. It was the beginning of a career of protest that led ultimately to the House of Commons. In vigorous—indeed, often violent—speeches he attacked the manufacturing interests, blaming them for the Poor Laws and wretched factory conditions. Ferrand had been in Parliament only a short time before he singled out for attack the new member for Stockport, Richard Cobden, who had already gained a reputation as a leader of the Anti-Corn Law League. Ferrand charged that every farthing Cobden had gained by the cotton trade 'was dyed in the blood of the poor'.[39] This was strong stuff: it indicated the debating style which would bring an occasional rebuke from the Speaker. It further indicated the passion (if not the reason) that informed the opposition to the Poor Laws.

Ferrand and his colleagues objected to the new Poor Law on three general grounds. First, they claimed that to place the administration of the Poor Laws in a centralised body such as the Poor Law Commission was an infringement of local rights. Second, they claimed that the Commission lacked specific knowledge of local conditions and tended to adopt an inflexible approach to the problems of poor relief. Third, they charged that the new Poor Law oppressed the poor, was inhumane and even unchristian. Practices such as the discontinuance of outdoor relief, the separation of families, arbitrary punishment, and bad food were cited in evidence. Abuses in the new Poor Law no doubt existed: they were probably inevitable in any extensive system of poor relief. But it seems that Ferrand was overstating his case. Workhouse provisions were not always rigorously enforced. More specifically, it seems that outdoor relief was continued in some Poor Law unions, directly contravening the instructions of the Poor Law Commission. The Commission, in fact, could reprimand and inspect, but could not compel unions to follow its instructions.

The ministry was unmoved by Ferrand's attacks. Graham, defending ministerial policy, declared that local management of poor relief was guaranteed by the Poor Law Guardians. The central body only guided policy to ensure certain standards of uniformity. This did not mean rigidity, Graham claimed, for the Poor Law system was not 'an unbending cast-iron system' but a 'plastic system'.[40] As proof of flexibility, he cited the Poor Law Commission's policy with regard to the workhouse test, the most controversial provision of the new Poor Law. Graham believed that test to be the most efficacious mode of determining real destitution: no workman would willingly place himself in the workhouse unless his need were great enough. Yet 'it would be cruel in the extreme', Graham declared, if the workhouse test were made the universal rule. Practically, there were extensive exceptions. Of 345,656 able-bodied adults relieved in 1841, only 65,467 were relieved in the workhouse. As a further defence of the new Poor Law, Graham pointed to the reduction in the number of those receiving relief. In 1803, 12 percent of the population were on poor relief: by 1841, this had dropped to only 8 percent. No one, suggested Graham, would want a return to the swollen relief rolls of the Elizabethan Poor Law system. At the conclusion of the Poor Law debates of 1842, the ministry proposed, and Parliament accepted, an extension of the Poor Law Commission for another five years. The only other Poor Law legislation of importance was the Poor Law Amendment Act of 1844. It enacted a new law of bastardy, regulated more clearly the relations of pauper apprentices and their masters, altered the mode of voting for Guardians and their qualifications for office, and sponsored district pauper schools. Although sporadic anti-Poor Law opposition continued during the life of the ministry, it never weakened ministerial determination to maintain the new Poor Law system.

More serious conflicts over social legislation occurred between the ministry and a small group of socially concerned Conservative MPs. These 'Tory paternalists' have been charged with sentimentalism and advocating unconstructive programmes. They nevertheless commanded a certain respect for their devout Anglicanism and deeply held conservatism. Motivated by a strong humanitarianism, they were more ready than their colleagues to extend the role of the state in correcting social injustice. Foremost among them was Anthony Ashley Cooper, Lord Ashley, whose reputation for sincerity and moral probity gave his opinions an unusual influence in Parliament. Ashley's staunch independence and tenacity on behalf of the poor and disadvantaged often placed the ministry in a dilemma. On the one hand, they feared that too much governmental regulation would discourage entrepreneurial activity. On the other hand, the ministry could not allow profit-taking at the expense of public health and safety. It is not an uncommon dilemma for governments, but it was an especially acute one in an age of ostensible *laissez-faire*.

Ashley's independence was made clear early in the life of the ministry. On 7 June 1842, Ashley introduced in Parliament a bill limiting the employment of women and children in the mines. The need for regulation was justified by the evidence of an interim report (made public in May 1842) of a Royal Commission which Ashley himself had secured two years previously. The Commission was investigating the conditions of children working in all the important industries then exempted from government regulations, such as mining, and the earthenware, metal, porcelain, and dress-making industries. The Commissioners—the economist Thomas Tooke, the utilitarian reformer Southwood Smith, and two factory inspectors, Robert Saunders and Leonard Horner—were assiduous in their work. They revealed the abuse of child labour (and, incidentally, of female labour) to an extent never suspected by the public at large. The wealth of evidence, accompanied by pictures detailing it, was a shock to the public mind. The reaction was swift and unmistakably favourable to government action. Even such disparate journals as *The Quarterly Review* and the *Westminster Review* agreed on the need for action.

The ministry responded cautiously, however, to Ashley's bill. Admitting that some governmental intervention in this instance was 'indispensable', Graham nevertheless expressed reservations about its over-extension.[41] Ministerial reserve toward the bill was more in evidence in the House of Lords. In fact, as Wharncliffe told the Lords, the ministry had decided not to support the bill, although any member of the government might do so as an individual.[42] Freed from the constraints of a unified cabinet policy on the bill, Wellington and Wharncliffe voiced some opposition to it. Wellington objected to the way in which the Commission had collected its evidence, implying that it was not always reliable. Wharncliffe had more serious reservations. He thought Parliament was legislating 'on a sudden impulse' and criticised the House of Commons for not affording an opportunity to the mine owners to rebut the charges made against them. In spite of these criticisms, ministers were unwilling to defeat the proposal. Instead, amendments were allowed. Although the prohibition of women from underground work in mines and collieries remained intact, the Lords had lowered from 13 to 10 the age below which boys would be excluded from the mines. When the amended bill returned to the House of Commons, Ashley reluctantly accepted the amendment, declaring unhappily that he had 'sacrificed the children in order to save the women'.[43] Most ministers in the House of Commons eventually supported the amended bill, though tepidly. Peel, for example, spoke only once for the bill. Gladstone actually voted against it.

The ministry's unenthusiastic response to Ashley's bill did not mean that they were uninterested in improving the lot of the working man. There was, however, an obvious difference in motivation between Ashley's proposals and the ministry's own initiatives in social legislation. It was for Ashley a crusade. The ministry was much more concerned with the promotion of social and political order. The ministry's own factory proposals in the year following Ashley's initiatives of 1842 make this very clear. One of the important aims of the ministry's bill was to provide more educational opportunities for young factory workers. Factory schools had first been established in 1802 when the Health and Morals of Apprentices Act of that year provided for the daily instruction of textile factory apprentices. The principle of factory education was strengthened by the Factory Act of 1833 which gave inspectors authority over factory school-teachers. In both these acts, textile mills had been chosen because of the high proportion of children in their labour force. The aim of factory education was not only to provide basic skills in reading, writing, and arithmetic, but also—at least in the minds of some factory owners—to inculcate factory discipline. This was consistent with the dominant nineteenth-century attitude toward popular education, which viewed it primarily as an instrument of social control.

Graham believed as strongly as any in the efficacy of education as a means of social control. He emphasised the moral content of education, and thought primarily in terms of religious (or, more specifically, Anglican) education. He was convinced that the riots and disorders of the winter of 1842 were the result of a declining religious sentiment. Therefore, Parliament should 'rescue the rising generation in the manufacturing districts from the state of practical infidelity' in which they were placed.[44] Only if 'the education of the rising youth should be the peculiar care of the Government' could the moral tone of the nation be elevated.[45] As Graham well knew, the practical realisation of his aim would be difficult. For the state to sponsor religious training in the factory schools meant favouring the Church of England, at least to a degree.

In view of the anticipated difficulty, Graham took exceptional care in the drafting of the educational clauses of the proposed bill. He consulted two of the factory inspectors, Leonard Horner, who he believed had some influence with the dissenters, and Robert Saunders, who had the confidence of the Bishop of London. He also drew upon the educational expertise of James Kay-Shuttleworth. To ensure support among the Anglican hierarchy, he sent advance copies of the proposed bill to the Archbishop of Canterbury and the Bishops of Chester, London and Ripon. Presented to Parliament in March 1843, the bill provided a board of seven trustees for every factory school. Three of the trustees would be Anglican clergymen or churchwardens and two would be factory owners, chosen by local magistrates in Petty Sessions. The trustees would manage the school, including the appointment of its schoolmaster, subject to the approval of the bishop of the diocese in which the school was located. In addition to his normal teaching duties, the master would also be responsible for religious instruction. To disarm critics, Graham included a clause that would exempt children from religious instruction if their parents objected. But, as Graham admitted to Gladstone, the tenor of the Act was undoubtedly pro-Anglican: 'the Church has ample security that every master in the new schools will be a

Churchman, and that the teaching of the Holy Scripture . . . will necessarily be in conformity with his creed'.[46]

Opposition to the intent of the bill was swift. In Parliament, B. Hawes (Lambeth) claimed that, under the ministry's scheme, children would be 'wholly at the mercy of the Church'. [47] M. Phillips (Manchester) charged that it was nothing less than a plot to recruit members for the Church of England.[48] Outside Parliament, the fear of state-supported proselytism brought an unusual commonness of purpose among dissenting sects. An extra-parliamentary pressure group, the United Conference, co-ordinated dissenter opposition to the bill. Within two months, it had organised the presentation to Parliament of several thousand petitions, with over two million signatures. This outburst was even more hostile than the ministry had anticipated, and in June 1843 the educational clauses of the bill were withdrawn. In its failure to make the Church of England responsible for the education of England's manufacturing population, the Peel ministry witnessed the fading of Anglican hopes to reassert its claim as the effective church of the whole state.[49] Where the ministry had hoped to advance the cause of the Church, dissent had instead won a battle that consolidated its victory of 1828 when the Test and Corporation Acts were repealed.

Although the ministry withdrew the educational clauses, it intended to proceed with the remainder of its factory bill which contained provisions for regulating factory employees' hours of work. Opposition to the educational clauses had delayed the bill as a whole, however, and the ministry decided against introducing the remainder in the waning days of the parliamentary session of 1843. Not until February 1844 did Graham submit the truncated Factory Bill. It proposed reduced daily working hours of factory children (8–13 years of age) from 9 to 6½ hours, and increased their required hours in school from 2 to 3 hours daily. Effectively, factory children would be working only half a day, and spending a proportionately greater amount of time in school. Thus was created the 'half-timer', as the factory child was known thereafter. The proposed bill did not change the limitation on work hours of young persons (13–18 years of age): these remained twelve hours daily. The Act contained one further provision, an important one in that it altered the prevailing practice of factory legislation. Hitherto, Factory Acts had limited only the hours of work of children and young persons. The new bill proposed limitation of the hours of adult females as well, also to twelve hours daily. By its application to textile mills, the new proposal would extend considerably the precedent for the regulation of adult labour set by the Mines Act of 1842.

At first, it seemed that the House of Commons was disposed to accept the ministerial bill as presented. But on 15 March 1844, Ashley moved an amendment to reduce the twelve hours' limitation of young persons and women to ten hours daily. The introduction of the Ten Hours' Movement into the factory debate precipitated the most serious crisis in the life of the ministry to that time. As the debate on the ten hours' amendment developed over the next two months, the ministry was forced into a series of uncomfortable manoeuvres. At first, they argued against Ashley on economic grounds. They solicited advice from two of the factory inspectors, Horner and Saunders, the former of whom believed that a reduction to ten hours would mean a 25 percent reduction in wages because employers would be unwilling to pay a twelve hours' rate for ten hours' work. Respected economic theorists, such as Nassau Senior, held the same view. On the basis of this advice, Graham declared in the House of Commons that a reduction of two hours' work might harm British industry by reducing productivity, thus lowering profits and ultimately wages. Peel supported his Home Secretary. Peel claimed he would rather that women worked only eight hours daily. But it was 'utterly impossible' that commerce should be disregarded in the matter and that 'humanity and morality alone' should be considered.[50]

Not all members of the House were convinced. After all, the proposed legislation left unregulated adult male labour which would presumably work as long as it wished (although the ministry hinted that the limitation might indirectly have the effect of restricting male labour as well). Moreover, the historic trend of factory legislation had been to curtail long working days. Would another two hours make much difference? Some members thought not. For other members, political reasons were doubtless foremost in their support of Ashley. The agricultural interest, upset by the ministry's liberalised tariff policy and angered by the activities of the Anti-Corn Law League, saw an easy opportunity for revenge against the manufacturers. There was also doubtless some partisan motivation behind the sudden conversion of Lord John Russell, after so many years of opposition, to the Ten Hours' Movement.

This mixture of motives accounts for the surprising victory in committee of Ashley's amendment on 18 March 1844. It had been a close vote: 170–179. Ashley's amendment had a further hurdle to overcome a few days later, on 22 March, when the specific clause of the Ten Hours' Bill was presented. This time, however, the vote went against Ashley. To the confusion of all, the House also voted down a twelve hours' clause. The stage seemed ideally set for an eleven hours' compromise, and some of Ashley's supporters signalled that they would be willing to accept it. But the cabinet, with the exception of Gladstone and Wharncliffe, was adamant against any compromise. Peel maintained that parliamentary interference with the bill was 'wrong in itself' and that he was unwilling 'to add one tittle' to it.[51] After the decisive cabinet meeting on the morning of 25 March, the ministry made known its position to the House of Commons that afternoon. Graham was the spokesman. He announced the ministry's intention of bringing forward a new bill after the

Easter recess. It would not, he warned, be based on any compromise since the ministry was determined to maintain a twelve hours' limitation. He justified the ministry's position by declaring the dangers of 'legislative interference' with the free market for labour. Indeed, he declared, a ten hours' bill would be the beginning of what he called a 'Jack Cade system of legislation. . . .'[52]

Graham's remarks angered the House. Even cabinet colleagues thought he had gone too far. Gladstone thought it sounded like the speech of an 'ultradoctrinarian' and told Graham afterwards that it had been 'fearfully strong'.[53] Staunch Conservatives such as Sir Robert Inglis and W. Busfield Ferrand, who had voted with Ashley, objected to Graham's implication that they were legislative radicals. Furthermore, it was obvious that the principle of non-interference with labour, which Graham upheld, had long ago been breached, most recently by the ministry's own proposed legislation on adult female labour. When Graham resubmitted the bill after Easter, it was essentially the same as the old. He advanced a new argument in its favour, however. Should a ten hours' amendment pass, Graham said, he would 'seek a private station'.[54] In short, the ministry would resign. This brought the dissidents to heel. A few tried to save face by declaring their conversion to the ministry's point of view. H. G. Knight (Nottinghamshire), who had voted three times for Ashley, declared that 'nothing had occurred except time to inquire—time to reflect—time to get sober'.[55] But it was obvious that he was changing his vote because the ministry had cracked the whip. H. T. Liddell (North Durham) was more candid when he declared that while his sympathy was with Ashley, his confidence in the Ministry carried him the other way. Ashley's ten hours' amendment lost heavily, 297–159.

The ministry no doubt believed that there were economic reasons for maintaining a twelve hours' limitation. But Peel himself admitted that in practice there were only a few mills

in which workers had a twelve-hour day. Why not compromise, then? The reason lay in Peel's belief, shared by
Graham especially, that cabinet government and executive
action were the only effective way to carry on the growing
mass of public business. Peel explained his attitude in a letter
to Lady de Grey near the end of the 1844 session. 'There is
not time to confer with individuals, to soften down objections by personal conferences, to flatter vanity by showing
confidence and appearing to consult. . . .' He expected his
party to support, if necessary, every clause of designated
bills. As he put it to Lady de Grey: 'We must . . . presume
upon *confidence*. . . .'[56]

It is not surprising that Ashley's initiatives were more than
annoying to a ministry which felt so strongly about its
executive prerogatives. However, Ashley was not deterred
by the ministry's coolness. In 1845, he sponsored two other
pieces of major social legislation. The first concerned the
conditions of asylums and madhouses and the treatment of
their inmates. In 1842, Ashley had secured an Act of Parliament that empowered the Metropolitan Commissioners in
Lunacy to carry out a thorough inspection of all institutions
which housed the insane. As a Lunacy Commissioner of
fourteen years' standing, Ashley could effectively document
his plea. In 1844, the Commissioners' report was completed.
On the basis of its evidence, Ashley brought forward in
Parliament the following year two bills to reform the administrative machinery concerning the care of lunatics. The
general effect of the bills was to reconstruct the Metropolitan Commissioners in Lunacy by granting them wider powers of inspection, licensing, and reporting. It was a milestone
on the road away from the earlier notorious practices of
Bedlam and toward modern ideas of mental health services.

Ashley's second reform measure of 1845 grew out of the
Royal Commission on the employment of children. It will
be remembered that the Commission had investigated abuses
not only in mines and collieries, but in numerous other un-

regulated industries as well. Ashley was determined to extend governmental regulations over these exempted industries. He decided to concentrate on calico printing, a seasonal industry that during its busy times in spring and autumn worked its employees 12–14 hours, and often ran relays of workers at night. Since it was a textile-related industry, Ashley believed that the restrictions of work contained in the Factory Act of 1844 could be extended to it relatively easily. His proposal to limit the hours of women and children in calico printing, introduced to the House of Commons in February 1845, did not initially attract the support of the ministry. Graham, as ministerial spokesman, declared that the employment of children in calico printing was more necessary than in many other industries. For a seasonal industry, any limitation of hours at the busy season could cripple productivity and might mean 'a very large sacrifice of profits' on the part of the mill owners.[57] Graham did not, however, rule out the possibility of ministerial support for Ashley. In the following weeks, Graham sought advice on the possible effects of Ashley's proposal. On 22 March, he held an interview with the factory inspectors and instructed them to utilise the sub-inspectors in each district to gather information. He also received deputations from some of the mill masters. As a result of these discussions, the ministry decided that some regulation was necessary. The ministry agreed with those parts of Ashley's bill that provided education for children under thirteen, that prohibited labour of children less than eight years of age, and that prohibited night labour for women and children. The ministry did not agree to limit the hours of labour for children between eight and thirteen, however. With Ashley's acceptance of the ministry's counter-proposal, an effective compromise was reached and the measure passed into law.

A final area of social legislation, and one in which the ministry took important initiatives, was connected with railways. In the five years of Peel's administration, railway mileage nearly doubled, from 1,696 to 3,036 miles, the number of passengers carried rose from 24 to 44 million, and goods receipts rose from £1,559,000 to £2,840,000. So rapid had been its growth that the 'railway mania' threatened to bring chaos in the financial markets as investors feverishly sought to profit on railway shares. As railways pushed through the country, passengers' safety also became an issue. With the railway companies providing only rudimentary safety precautions, multiple accidents increased with every mile of track laid. In the single year 1841, there were 65 accidents resulting in 41 passenger deaths and 92 injuries. There were an additional 60 accidents among railway employees, resulting in 28 deaths and 36 injuries.[58] These statistics raised doubts in the minds of many about the wisdom of an inadequately regulated railway system.

In theory, the ministry strongly upheld *laissez-faire* with regard to railway development. Speaking in a parliamentary debate on railway passenger safety, Peel opposed a resolution by a private member that would have required a minimum distance between engine and passenger cars on moving trains. Peel argued that such a measure would increase, rather than diminish accidents. His reasoning was that railway companies would tend to become negligent once relieved of their responsibilities by the government. Peel thought 'the public might be trusted to take care of themselves'.[59]

Yet on other occasions the ministry took quite distinct steps in the direction of intervention. In February 1842, Gladstone (as Vice-President of the Board of Trade, the official most responsible for the railways in the House of Commons), brought in a bill that made more effective the existing inspection of railway lines prior to their opening to the public. Other provisions required that railway companies should report all accidents on their lines and improved some safety procedures. In 1844, the ministry introduced one of the most famous of all Railway Acts, designed specifically to promote the safety and convenience of third-class passengers. Third-class carriages were often open to the weather and scarcely fit for cattle. Some railways did not even carry third-class passengers in the belief that they were an uneconomical load. There was, furthermore, a great disparity of charges between the different railway companies. On the Liverpool and Manchester line, passengers were charged 16s 8d for 100 miles, while on the Glasgow and Greenock line they were charged only 2s 3d. Gladstone proposed that companies which derived one-third or more of their revenue from passengers (as a great majority of the companies did) were to run at least one train daily. The fare must be no more than 1d per mile, and the train must stop at every station and run at a speed of not less than 12 mph. Thus began the so-called 'parliamentary trains'. Further legislation ensured a higher standard of comfort and safety for passengers by licensing the Board of Trade to approve the construction of railway carriages. These provisions of the Railway Act of 1844 were the ministry's most successful efforts in railway legislation.

The ministry had less success in regulating the entrepreneurial side of railway development. Gladstone's Railway Act of 1844, which had introduced parliamentary trains, had also contained provisions for the regulation of boards of management of railway companies. 'The Railroad', Gladstone observed, 'had gone among individual traders very much like a triton among the minnows. . . .'[60] To prevent fraud and protect the public interest, Gladstone brought railway companies into his general scheme for the regulation of joint-stock companies. Furthermore, he proposed regulating railway companies in the same way that the Bank of England and the East India Company were regulated—that is, by review. If, at the end of fifteen years, the annual divisible profits on the paid-up share capital of any company equalled 10 percent, the government would have the option of revising the fares and charges of that company. Another provision would have allowed the government the option of purchasing any new railway line, whatever the profits.

If they had passed, these provisions would have been a remarkable extension of the principle of state intervention in the affairs of railways. It is not altogether clear how Gladstone could have justified such a measure, given the views of the ministry of which he was a member. Indeed, it seems that it was more a personal than a ministerial bill: many of Gladstone's cabinet colleagues opposed it.[61] Nor, as one would expect, was the railway interest enthusiastic. The *Railway Times* called Gladstone's proposal the 'Railway Plunder Bill.' In June 1844, a deputation representing nearly thirty railway companies expressed to Peel, Gladstone, and Lord Granville Somerset their firm opposition to the bill. The pressure of the railway interest had its effect. On 22 July 1844, Gladstone made an apologetic speech to the House of Commons in which he announced the deletion of some twenty clauses of the original bill. Those clauses had been originally inserted, Gladstone claimed, 'to give satisfaction to the railway proprietors'. However, Gladstone continued, 'a body of Gentlemen connected with railways took a different view of the matter'. Since it had not been his intention to discourage the application of capital to railway enterprises, he had acquiesced in the suggested alterations 'without reluctance'. Gladstone assured the House that there had been no intention on the part of the ministry to become the manager of the railways. Rather, the intention of the bill had been to reserve the right of the legislature to act on behalf of the public.[62] Gladstone's somewhat awkward retractions did not conceal the fact that the ministry had retreated in the face of the opposition of the railway interest.

The influence of the railway interest may be further illustrated in the fate of the Railway Board, established in August 1844. Presided over by Lord Dalhousie, Vice-President of the Board of Trade since Gladstone's promotion in 1843, its aim was to expedite the passage of railway bills through the House of Commons. Previously, each railway line had to be sanctioned by the whole of Parliament. In 1840, 24 Railway Acts had been approved by Parliament; by 1845, the number had risen to 121, and by 1846 to 272.[63] Unless some system could be devised for controlling the applications, the business of Parliament would become impossibly cumbersome. The Railway Board was to receive the applications from the railway companies and to make recommendations as to which line should be passed, postponed, or rejected. During the parliamentary recess of 1844, the Board was hard at work, making its recommendations through an ambitious series of reports. Early in the parliamentary session of 1845, however, there were strong objections raised against the operations of the Railway Board. Some felt that the Board was assuming too much authority and usurping the right of parliamentary review over railway applications. Even the radical Thomas Wakley, who had previously supported stringent governmental regulation of the railways, complained of what he called the 'secret transactions' of the Board.[64] Viscount Howick had a similar complaint. He understood that the Board was to offer advice and provide information only. Howick was fearful that the decisions of the Board about prospective railway lines might be too often regarded as final: all such decisions should come before the House for authorisation. But Howick had another reason for opposing the Board—one that might well have motivated others. In a statement to the House of Commons, he candidly admitted that he had been interested in a railway line that had been unfavourably viewed by the Board.[65] The fact that Howick unabashedly declared his interest probably tells much about the sympathetic audience he expected to find in the House.[66]

There was no defence of the Board among the ministers. When Peel withdrew his support for the Board's continuance in 1845, its fate was sealed. It had lasted scarcely a year. The demise of the Board removed an impartial panel which might have placed railway development above the interplay of private interest. The collapse of the Railway Board and, indeed, of much of the ministry's railway policy, has since been regarded as an opportunity lost. Not for a further two decades was there an attempt on the part of government to exert effective control over the railways. Given the general climate of opinion on social questions in the Peel ministry and the tendency to confine its responses to administrative reform, perhaps such a policy was inevitable.

In concluding this discussion of the Peel ministry's social legislation, a useful purpose may be served by placing it within the context of a debate among historians about the growth of government in the first half of the nineteenth century. Broadly speaking, there are two schools of thought, the theorists and the empiricists. The theorists claim that the impetus for the growth of governmental intervention derived from Bentham and his disciples. Bentham laid the philosophical foundation for intervention in his principle of utility. Benthamite publicists popularised the theory, and Benthamite civil servants exercised their influence within government circles to enact utilitarian reforms. The empiricists deny the importance of theory. They believe that governments for the most part merely respond to the pressure of events. This accounts for Britain's erratic and piecemeal reformism.[67]

How well does each model fit Peel's ministry? It cannot be claimed that the ministers were Benthamites or Benthamite sympathisers. But the theorists are not likely to make such a claim. They emphasise the influence of civil servants upon governments of the day. It is certainly true that the Peel ministry relied upon the renowned investigative powers of Benthamite officials. The Royal Commission on children's employment contained at least one well-known utilitarian reformer, Southwood Smith, as well as one factory inspector, Horner, who was utilitarian in sympathy. Horner's advice was also sought by Graham during the drafting of the factory legislation of 1843. But it will be remembered that Horner advised a cautious policy in restricting the working day, not one that advocated a further extension of governmental intervention. Indeed, it was Ashley, hardly a Benthamite, who urged a greater intervention in the affairs of the mill owners.

On balance, the empiricist model is a better guide to the Peel ministry. Peel and his colleagues were not root-and-branch social reformers, acting on a rational plan of governmental intervention. They were too inhibited by their belief in the limits of human intelligence and energy to think that comprehensive government programmes might solve complex social problems. They were conscious of the need to balance interests—economic, religious, or political—and were fearful of tipping the balance unfavourably against any single interest. They felt their way slowly, nudged forward on occasion by one interest or deflected elsewhere by another. Perhaps the ministry may best be characterised in its social policy as grand masters of the science of muddling through, an admirable practice in the opinion of some, and one not to be despised.

3 IRELAND:
CLOUD IN THE WEST

Although the financial and social questions posed numerous difficult problems for the ministry, Peel and his colleagues felt reasonably confident that answers could be found. Ministerial confidence seemed often to wane, however, before another great question of the day—Ireland. The Irish question had contributed much to the troubled days of previous administrations, and Peel's administration was not to be spared its share as the Repeal Movement in Ireland reached crisis proportions during the early 1840s.

The administration's Irish policy may be seen as undergoing three distinct phases. The first phase, extending from 1841 to mid-1843, was characterised by what might be termed a benign neglect. Indeed, it seemed that the ministry lacked an Irish policy during these two years. Under the pressure of Irish events, however, the last half of 1843 witnessed a reversal of ministerial inactivity as the passage of an Arms Bill and the dismissal of Irish magistrates initiated a policy of coercion. The third phase, from 1844 to the end of the ministry, was characterised by conciliatory legislation as the ministry sought to promote the welfare of Ireland through the passage of important educational and religious measures.

The reason for the ministry's initial inactivity was simple: Ireland was superficially tranquil. The activities of the secret societies of the Irish peasantry—such as the Rockites and the Ribbandmen—were at a low ebb. Also, the influence of Ireland's only national leader of stature, Daniel O'Connell, appeared to be waning. His Repeal Association, dedicated

to repealing the Act of Union with Britain, seemed mori-
bund. At the general election of 1841, O'Connell, standing as
a repealer for the City of Dublin, was defeated—although
he was later returned for Cork. There were only seventeen
other repealers returned with O'Connell in 1841, representing
a steady decline since 1832, when thirty-eight repealers had
been returned to Parliament. Without the Whigs in office,
O'Connell's influence was bound to suffer an eclipse. It
seemed, at least to the British, that the best days of the ageing O'Connell were over. Indeed, *The Times* could write
with satisfaction in 1842 that 'the game is up with the old
man' for he had sunk into 'profound obscurity'.[1]

Events were to prove that O'Connell's epitaph as a public
man was premature. His stature in Ireland remained high.
In 1841 he became Lord Mayor of Dublin, the first Catholic
in that office since the time of James II. He had never ceased
his efforts to organise from the grass roots a National Repeal
Movement. He worked closely with Richard Barrett, editor
of *The Pilot*, a Dublin newspaper which became the unoffi-
cial mouthpiece of repeal. He also maintained contact with
John MacHale, the Catholic Archbishop of Tuam. Furthermore, in working out the arrangements for repeal meetings,
he continually urged his agents to secure the approval of the
Catholic clergy, whose influence on political questions was
steadily increasing. By early 1843, O'Connell's efforts bore
fruit. In February, O'Connell, then a Dublin alderman,
sponsored a repeal motion in the Dublin corporation. Its
passage, by a vote of 41-15, was nothing less than a sensation.
As the Anglican, Conservative, and virulently anti-repeal
Dublin Evening Mail observed on 6 March 1843, repeal had
made 'an immense as well as a rapid stride' by advancing
'from the platform of a seditious assembly to the council-
table of legitimate municipal government. . . .' The weekly
meetings of the Repeal Association, which had been held in
the Dublin Corn Exchange, now attracted more notice.
The repeal 'rent'—contributions to the Association—

increased. A national campaign of repeal meetings in every county in Ireland was initiated. O'Connell reminded his audiences throughout Ireland that Peel and Wellington had responded to public pressure in granting Catholic Emancipation in 1829. Why not again?

The repeal meetings were an unqualified success in attracting crowds. In August 1843, there were a reported 200,000 to 300,000 present at Castlebar, Co Mayo; 200,000 at Baltinglass, Co Wicklow; 350,000 at Roscommon; and, at the largest meeting of all, one million at Tara. Even allowing for considerable exaggeration (some estimates put the Tara meeting at only 500,000), these were impressive numbers. Named 'monster meetings' by *The Times*, they seemed to give substance to O'Connell's claim that Ireland was becoming one nation under the repeal agitation. Some of the most respected leaders in Ireland—both lay and clerical— spoke at the meetings. They included MacHale of Tuam, the Bishop of Meath, the Bishop of Ardagh, and numerous other clergymen. The Bishop of Ardagh, the Rt Rev Dr Higgins, claimed at the Mullingar meeting—to tumultuous applause— that all the Roman Catholic bishops favoured repeal.[2] The Bishop of Killala, the Rt Rev Dr Feeny, who chaired the meeting at Ballina, declared that 'Repeal can alone satisfy an oppressed nation'.[3] At Ballingarry, Archdean Fitzgerald declared that: 'The Repeal of the Union will make Ireland take her place among the nations.'[4] Among the repeal members of Parliament who spoke at various meetings were Henry Grattan, MP for Meath; J. P. Somers, MP for Sligo; Robert Dillon Browne, MP for Co Mayo; Mark Blake, MP for Co Mayo; John J. Bodkin, MP for Galway; and O'Connell's son, John, MP for Kilkenny.

O'Connell maintained that repeal did not mean separation from Britain, but that it did mean an Irish parliament and self-government. On 21 July 1843, the O'Connellite *Pilot* put the demands of the repealers thus: 'We agitate for a Domestic Legislature, with adequate powers, and those powers guaranteed, which shall have full dominion over the management of our domestic concerns, and the development and appropriation of our productive capacities.' Too often had the imperial Parliament neglected Irish interests. An Irish parliament, O'Connell promised, would abolish tithe rent-charges, revise the poor relief system, and assure fixity of tenure. Repealers throughout Ireland were not slow to develop the theme. At Kells, Nicholas Boylan, JP, promised that an Irish parliament would sponsor drainage projects and railways.[5] Indeed, some repealers seemed to think that repeal and an Irish parliament would right every wrong. All the 'giant grievances under which we groan are the spawn of the detested union', declared the Very Rev Dr M'Ginnis at Clones.[6]

The aspirations of the repealers revealed at their meetings suggest why the movement should have suddenly caught fire in 1843. Recurring economic and religious grievances had come to a head. Economic trends, detrimental to industrial development, were especially worrying to Irish merchants. Unlike most other countries, Ireland was becoming increasingly rural. Few of the major towns—apart from Belfast and Dublin—grew between 1821 and 1841. Some smaller centres stagnated. The severe economic slump of the early 1840s revealed the inadequate resources at Ireland's command. Whereas England had the means to overcome the economic downturn, Ireland had not. Indeed, Irish investment tended to flow outward toward the greater opportunities in England. Thus, great enterprises of the age such as railways were woefully lagging in Ireland. By 1845, there were only seventy miles of railway open in Ireland. But when the Irish looked to Parliament for aid, they were not infrequently rebuffed. When, for example, the Whigs in the late 1830s enacted legislation that would have assumed more state responsibility for the development of Irish railways, the measure was so strongly attacked—not least by Sir Robert Peel—that it was eventually dropped. Peel had not changed his mind upon assuming office. When Fisher Stephen French, MP for Roscommon, attempted to revive in Parliament the idea of state aid for Irish railways, Peel was unsympathetic.[7] Setting himself against the view that railways were necessarily a permanent benefit to Ireland, Peel declared that the granting of public money for railways in Ireland would be a 'fatal gift' because it would utilise Irish labourers only temporarily. Once the railways had been completed and labourers could find no other employment, Peel maintained that Ireland's misery would be compounded. In short, Peel informed the House of Commons, unless railway construction in Ireland were undertaken on the same principle as in England—that is, by private enterprise—it 'ought not to be undertaken at all'.[8] Peel was not opposed to the construction of Irish railways, but he feared that large expenditures on public works would lead to abuse and jobbery. He preferred to authorise loans to Irish railway companies through the Exchequer Bill Loan Commissioners, which had extended loans for public works since 1817.[9] This approach to railway construction, however, was predicated upon a level of indigenous private enterprise that simply did not exist in Ireland.

Agricultural development in Ireland faced as many problems as industrial development. Though Ireland was fertile, agricultural improvement was hindered by absentee landlords and an insecurity of tenure that discouraged tenant farmers from undertaking even the simplest manuring and drainage practices. In England a tenant farmer was an entrepreneurial partner with his landlord. He was a small capitalist who cultivated his farm for profit and was responsible for the payment of wages and the organisation of the work of farm labourers who were his employees. But in Ireland, divisions of interest and religion too often made the landlord and his tenants bitter foes, preventing any possibility of an economic partnership. Repealers believed that an Irish parliament would find a solution to the land problem

sooner than the distant imperial Parliament in which, to
their way of thinking, too many absentee landlords sat.

A further source of repeal strength lay in the sense of
grievance among Catholics. An established Anglican Church
of Ireland ministered to the needs of scarcely 20 percent of
the population. Acquiescence in this state of affairs by the
Roman Catholic majority was wearing thin by the 1840s. The
first half of the nineteenth century was an age of rehabilita-
tion for Irish Catholicism. Churches were put into repair,
cathedrals were begun, parish schools were started, and
the National Seminary at Maynooth grew in importance.
For many Catholics, the repeal movement was a way of
demonstrating support for their faith. Not all repealers were
Catholics, however. So pervasive had repeal sentiment become by the early 1840s that some Protestant Irishmen
were attracted into its ranks. Among these were Thomas O.
Davis, a leader of the Young Ireland movement, and William
Smith O'Brien, MP for Limerick, who became a member of
the Repeal Association in 1843.

The strength of the repeal movement by the summer of
1843 caused growing alarm among its opponents. The organ
of the extreme Protestants, the *Dublin Evening Mail*, became
critical of the Peel ministry for not acting against the repeal
meetings. Opposition was also building in England against
the ministry's quiescent Irish policy. In May, a deputation
of Protestant peers urged upon Peel and Graham a proclamation against demonstrations in Ireland. In the same
month, *The Times* suggested a 'firm and determined' policy
for an agitated Ireland. By early June, *The Times* was convinced that Ireland was 'on the verge of rebellion', and by
July it harshly condemned the ministry, whose 'wits seem
fairly to have departed in this crisis'.

These criticisms of the ministry were somewhat unfair.
Ireland was becoming a matter of deep concern, as cabinet
memoranda and correspondence indicate. The ministry was
especially fearful that the largely Catholic repeal meetings
would call into opposition the Protestant Orange Societies,

which had been banned in the 1830s. Collision between the two could bring Ireland to the brink of civil war. But direct action against the repealers was difficult. In the first place, no laws had been broken: the meetings were careful not to breach the peace. In fact, O'Connell warned his followers at virtually every meeting against violence of any kind. The ministry realised that suppression of peaceable assemblies might alienate moderate Irishmen in whom the ministry placed its hopes. Therefore, in spite of Wellington's request that the ministry should put down 'the evil of these mob meetings',[10] Peel believed that nothing could be done until evidence of illegality was produced.

A second difficulty for the ministry was the internal division in its Irish administration. The Lord Lieutenant was Earl de Grey, a man unsympathetic to Irish aspirations and ultra-Protestant in his inclinations. Most other important Irish officials were also partisan Protestants. Edward Lucas, for example, the Under-Secretary, was an Irish Protestant landowner. Edward Sugden, the Lord Chancellor, as a member of Parliament in 1828 (during the debate on the Clare by-election), had advocated the exclusion of O'Connell from the House of Commons. The Chief Secretary, Lord Eliot, was very different in outlook, and believed from the first that ministerial policy should be conciliatory toward Ireland. It is not entirely clear why Peel should have appointed men of disparate views to such sensitive posts. Perhaps it was his way of striking a balance between coercion and conciliation.[11] He may also have hoped to bring the increasingly vociferous coercionist block of Tory peers under better control by co-opting de Grey. But the effect on the Irish administration was to give it a Protestant enough flavour to be distasteful to Catholics, yet Catholic enough (in the person of Lord Eliot) to alienate the most fervent Protestants. More important clashes between de Grey and Eliot grew as the repeal crisis deepened, weakening the ministry's potential for decisive action in Ireland.

Faced with a divided Irish administration, the cunning of

O'Connell, and Protestant fears, the ministry hardened its attitude. If it could not act against the repeal meetings, it was not without some recourse. Adopting an uncompromising position as a warning to the repealers, Peel declared in the House of Commons that, rather than allow 'the dismemberment of this empire', the ministry was prepared for civil war.[12] In late May 1843, the ministry introduced an Arms Bill imposing a tighter control on the traffic in Irish weapons. After frequently caustic exchanges on the state of Ireland during the extensive debates that followed, the measure was passed. Also in late May, to the delight of the Duke of Wellington, the cabinet resumed recruiting for the army. As Graham wrote to de Grey, Wellington had convinced the cabinet that they must prepare for '"La Grande Guerre" in Ireland. . . .'[13] Reinforcements were sent to Ireland, bringing the total military establishment there to its highest level in sixteen years. The Dublin garrison alone mustered nearly 4,600 men, and numerous other units were stationed throughout Ireland. By October 1843, there were some 34,000 troops there.

These coercive measures on the part of the ministry did not, however, stop the repeal meetings. Indeed, the military preparations merely provided O'Connell with an attractive topic for his speeches. At Mallow, for example, O'Connell reminded his audience of Cromwell's massacre of the ladies of Wexford and, to good effect, drew implicit parallels: 'I tell you this—300 of the grace and beauty, and virtue of Wexford were slaughtered by the English ruffians—Sacred Heaven! (tremendous sensation and cries of "Oh, oh") I am not at all imaginative when I talk of the possibility of such occurrences anew. . . .'[14] This was not the only occasion when analogies were drawn between Cromwell and Wellington.

In another action, the government played into the repealers' hands. A minor civil servant, an Ordnance Clerk of Works at Enniskillen, was dismissed in late May for attend-

ing a repeal meeting at Kells in Co Meath. Soon afterward,
Lord Ffrench, a Galway magistrate, was relieved of his
commission for announcing his intention to attend a repeal
meeting. By the end of May some fourteen magistrates had
been dismissed. Eventually the number rose to twenty-four
including several members of Parliament. The man responsible was the Lord Chancellor, Sugden, who had acted without consultation. It was a clumsy and questionable action,
for in his letters of dismissal Sugden admitted that the repeal
meetings were not illegal, but merely had a 'tendency to
outrage'. The dismissals were universally condemned, even
by the *Dublin Evening Mail.* Peel and Graham were not
opposed to dismissing repeal magistrates, but they were
displeased that Sugden had not taken the preliminary step
of issuing a general proclamation against the attendance of
magistrates at repeal meetings. Had Sugden issued a proclamation beforehand, the dismissals would have been, in
Graham's opinion, 'safe and easy': without it, Sugden's
action was 'not so direct or intelligible'.[15] Unhappy as they
were in private about the dismissals, the cabinet felt bound
to support Sugden in public. In Ireland, the dismissed
magistrates wore their removal as a badge of honour. They
were referred to collectively as 'Sugden's Martyrs' or as the
'Repeal Martyrs'. The whole episode was undoubtedly
damaging to the ministry and may well have driven some
moderate men into the ranks of the repealers.

The ministry's opportunity to act against the repeal
meetings came, as they had hoped, through the growing
militancy in the language of the repealers.[16] Although
O'Connell ostensibly did not abandon constitutional and
peaceful means of achieving repeal, military references as
well as separatist implications crept into his speeches. The
great meeting at Tara (the seat of the ancient Irish kings)
heard O'Connell declare that from there once emanated
'the legal authority' of the island, which included the
power of 'concentrating the force of the entire nation for the

purpose of national defence'.[17] At the Longrhea meeting a
few weeks later, Richard Barret of *The Pilot* reminded his
audience of their aim: 'We must agitate until we get domestic, and therefore not alien, legislation—peacefully, if per-
mitted.'[18] At the repeal meeting at Clifden, Connemara,
appeared the first 'peasant cavalry' (as *The Pilot* termed
them), a troop of some five to six hundred horsemen who
had ridden in procession to the meeting. R. Dillon Browne
called favourable attention to these men, 'who were determined to fight the battle of their country'. O'Connell, too,
praised what he called the 'mountaineer cavalry'. He also
drew further inferences from the whole series of mass meetings, claiming that 'more men of the fighting age (cheers)
than had ever made a declaration for any other country in
the world, had met together in Ireland to denounce the
Legislative Union.'[19]

A further disturbing development was O'Connell's announcement in early October at the Mullaghmast meeting
that he was forming a plan for an Irish House of Commons
—a plan he hoped would be realised within three weeks.
It was also announced that the repealers had instituted a new
court system in Ireland, termed arbitration courts, designed
to replace the English-dominated hierarchy of the Irish legal
system. In describing the first sitting of the new court system
at Blackrock, the repealist *Freeman's Journal* was plain as
to its intention: 'A great lesson is being taught to the Irish
people. They are by the introduction of the Repeal arbitration courts shown the practicability and the value of
taking the administration of the laws as well as their formation into their own hands. . . .'[20] The last straw for the
government was the announcement of a mass meeting
scheduled for 8 October at Clontarf, where the Irish had
defeated the Danes a century before the English invasion.
Apart from the martial associations of Clontarf among Irishmen, the announcements of the meeting were couched in more
combative phrases than ever before, including the term
'Repeal Cavalry'.

The ministry decided to act firmly. Since Earl de Grey, the Lord Lieutenant, was already in England, it was an easy matter for Peel and Graham to confer with him. This was done on 3 and 4 October. It was decided that the Clontarf meeting should be suppressed, by force if necessary, and that O'Connell and the leaders of the Repeal Association should be apprehended and charged with treasonable conspiracy. Graham, in the meantime, would undertake such military preparations as might be necessary. The proclamation against Clontarf was announced on 7 October upon de Grey's return to Ireland. O'Connell acquiesced immediately, urging upon his followers the continuance of legal and peaceful means to repeal. Within a week O'Connell and several others were arrested. The trial was postponed until the following year. Initially found guilty, O'Connell was released in 1844 on appeal to the House of Lords. Meanwhile the repeal movement, without a recognised leader, had been weakened. It never again reached the heights of 1843, and by 1846 the holocaust of the famine had engulfed it. The final collapse of the Repeal Association in 1848 marked the end of this phase of the movement for Irish independence.

With the threat of repeal easing in late 1843, the opportunity was provided for a new approach to Irish matters. The ministry realised that coercion could not be maintained indefinitely. For a variety of reasons, however, the options open to the ministry were limited. Economic grievances, especially, were thought to be beyond the scope of government action. As we have seen, Peel was opposed to state aid for railway construction. Nor was the ministry willing to oversee any major alteration of the Irish land system. As Graham declared in the House of Commons, the ministry would not countenance any reform that would interfere with property rights. A settlement of the religious question was also largely beyond the ministry's powers. The Conservative party could not alter the Church of Ireland without serious electoral consequences. Former Whigs such as

Stanley and Graham had originally joined the Conservatives partly because of the Whig attack upon the Irish
church in the 1830s. It was unlikely that they would reverse
themselves. In spite of these limitations, the ministry was
determined to pursue a policy of conciliation. The necessity
of this task was put by Graham in the grimmest of terms:
'If Ireland be not reconciled to Great Britain, she will destroy
us and open a breach in our defences through which our
foreign enemies will ultimately triumph.'[21] Only by winning
the good will of the majority of Irishmen—that is, of Catholic Irishmen—could loyalty to the Union be assured.

Conciliation of Catholic Ireland proceeded along several
lines. The ministry offered more positions of political
responsibility to Irish Catholics, improved clerical and
secular educational facilities, and encouraged the solvency
of Catholic institutions. It also attempted a reform of the
Irish franchise and a revision of the laws regarding land
occupation. Each of these will be discussed below.

It had long been an Irish complaint that Irishmen were
too often excluded from official circles at Dublin. In the
parliamentary debate on the state of Ireland in the summer
of 1843, W. Smith O'Brien had charged that Catholic
Emancipation could never be fully realised as long as religion
remained a bar to office. He cited the major appointments
in the Irish government, beginning with de Grey: of these,
twenty-three were held by Protestants and only three were
held by Catholics.[22] Peel felt the justice of this charge. In
a series of letters during the summer of 1843, Peel urged on a
reluctant de Grey the appointment of Catholics to vacant
posts even if, in some cases, the most qualified candidate
might be Protestant. As Peel explained to de Grey, unless
Irish Catholics felt an equal chance of royal favour, the
opening of civil privileges remained 'a dead letter'. In that
case, said Peel, 'we have done nothing by the removal of
disabilities but organise a band of mischievous dema-
gogues'.[23]

The government's liberal appointments policy was not an easy route to conciliation, however. De Grey was jealous of the patronage power in his hands and resentful of any inter-ference—even, it would seem, from Peel. Irish Protestants would be unlikely to applaud a policy which favoured Catholics; nor was there any guarantee that Catholics would accept the government's belated generosity with patronage. A perfect example of the government's difficulties was the affair of John Howley. When the judicial post of Third Sergeant fell vacant in the summer of 1843, Peel suggested to de Grey the appointment of Howley, a moder-ate Catholic barrister. The position was of some importance, falling third in precedence behind the Attorney-General and the Solicitor-General in the Irish court system. De Grey resisted the appointment, and declared that conciliation was 'a chimera'.[24] But Peel persisted and Howley was appointed. The reception of this news in Ireland was less than favour-able. It seems that Howley, who had been the Assistant Barrister for Tipperary before his elevation, had no standing in Ireland. It was too plain that his religion had been the reason for his appointment. The *Dublin Evening Mail* was outraged because more qualified Tory members of the bar had been overlooked.[25] The Catholic papers were also dis-pleased. On 1 September 1843 the *Freeman's Journal* denounced the 'shallow artifice' of the appointment, declar-ing that it was 'insulting' to Ireland. *The Pilot* condemned the appointment the same day in more colourful language, denouncing Howley as 'one of the Pope's bad bargains'. It was not an auspicious beginning to conciliation.

In Peel's mind, the key to conciliation lay with the Catho-lic clergy. The clergy had been prominent during the repeal agitation, and Peel was determined to win their loyalty to the Union. Cabinet discussion as to possible courses of ac-tion began in late 1843. Peel, Graham, and Stanley were generally agreed that the state must bear a greater responsi-bility for the education and maintenance of the clergy. This meant a review of ministerial policy toward the Royal College of St Patrick at Maynooth in Co Kildare. Maynooth was the national seminary for Catholic priests, established by the Irish parliament in 1795 as a means of luring the Irish clergy away from their traditional training in French seminaries, a potentially subversive education in the France of the Revolution. After the Union, the practice of supporting Maynooth from public funds continued, but by the 1840s the amount allocated was clearly inadequate. Fixed in 1808 at £9,250 annually, it had not been raised since. Successive governments' neglect of the facilities and educational standards at Maynooth alienated and embittered the clergy who studied there.

The cabinet's willingness to review Maynooth was a reversal of opinion. In 1842, Lord Eliot had urged an inquiry into Maynooth, but the cabinet had turned down his suggestion. Informing Eliot of the cabinet's decision, Peel had written of their reluctance to disturb the existing tranquillity.[26] Now that O'Connell's repeal meetings had ruffled the religious calm, that reason could no longer be advanced. The whole matter involved a delicate balancing act. If nothing were done for Maynooth, the success of conciliation could be jeopardised. Yet if something were done, the ministry might encounter what Graham called an 'invincible repugnance' from British Protestantism.[27]

Of more immediate concern to Peel was the discovery of ministerial divisions over Maynooth. When the subject was discussed at cabinet meetings early in the parliamentary session of 1844, Goulburn and Graham expressed some reservations. Gladstone was opposed outright to any increase in the Maynooth grant. He thought that any improvement in Ireland by such a scheme would be purely 'secondary', and that the whole idea was 'visionary'.[28] Gladstone's real difficulty with Maynooth proved to be a concern for his own reputation. In 1838, he had written *The State in its Relations with the Church*, which had upheld the principle that the state was bound to support the established church and no other. Maynooth violated that principle. If he supported any extension of state aid to Maynooth, Gladstone feared that his consistency would be impugned. Individual and collective cabinet appeals did not dissuade Gladstone, who threatened resignation if the ministry persisted. Unable to resolve its differences, the cabinet postponed any decision. Peel probably hoped that the difficulty could be resolved in time.

With action on Maynooth precluded for the moment, the ministry turned to other measures of conciliation. The Charitable Bequests and Donations Bill, introduced in 1844, placed Catholic clergy in Ireland on a more equitable financial footing. Existing law and practice hindered private endowment of Catholic chapels and benefices by ensuring that all members of the Board of Charitable Donations and Bequests were Protestants. Thus Catholic testators had no guarantee that their bequests would go to those Catholic institutions they designated. This exacerbated the inequities of clerical maintenance in Ireland. Whereas the Church of Ireland was well endowed, the Roman Catholic clergy were dependent upon a voluntary system of customary offerings and dues given by their (usually impoverished) parishioners. The proposed bill—sponsored, as Graham candidly admitted, as a 'peace-offering'—guaranteed an equal voice to Catholics on the Board. Encouragement of private endowments to Catholic institutions might reduce the disparity between the poverty of Catholic institutions and the prosperity of Anglican ones. The bill had an easy passage in Parliament, with Lord John himself approving it.

In Ireland, however, the legislation encountered opposition from the repeal leaders, especially MacHale of Tuam and the recently released O'Connell. They apparently feared that it would detract from repeal by removing genuine grievances. Campaigning among the clergy, they advocated non-cooperation with the new Board. To deflect the cam-

paign, the Irish executive entered into direct negotiations
with the Catholic hierarchy. Fortunately for the ministry,
Earl de Grey had resigned in May 1844, on grounds of
health, and his place had been taken by Lord Heytesbury.
A career diplomat and a man uninterested in promoting
either side in the sectarian strife, Heytesbury won the confidence of the hierarchy. A basis for agreement lay in the
fact that with only one exception (MacHale of Tuam, not
surprisingly), the hierarchy had petitioned the previous
Whig administration for just those concessions granted by
the Peel ministry under the new legislation. They could now
scarcely refuse what they themselves had so recently sought.
Nor could the Catholic hierarchy, well aware of the financial
plight of their church, turn aside support even if it came from
the coffers of an officially Protestant state. After protracted
discussions, a majority of the hierarchy agreed to cooperate
in the execution of the new bill. It was an important victory
for the ministry's policy of conciliation.

The ministry fared less well in two other attempts at conciliation. The first was an attempted reform of the Irish
franchise, introduced in April 1844. It would enfranchise the
five pound freeholder and remedy certain defects of the legal
machinery. But electoral reform, even at the best of times,
was a contentious issue. Conservatives thought the bill would
promote democratic tendencies by lowering the county franchise. Irish liberals and repealers, on the other hand, feared
it would place the newly enfranchised rural poor at the dis-
posal of their landlords on election day. This combined
assault doomed the bill, and it was withdrawn in June 1844.

A second ministerial failure related to land occupation.
In November 1843, the ministry appointed a commission
to consider the law and practice of land occupation in
Ireland. Named the Devon Commission after its chairman,
Lord Devon, it worked throughout the session of 1844, con-
ducting interviews and collecting evidence in Ireland. Fin-
ishing its task in 1845, the Commission published its find-

ings in four massive volumes.[29] As Stanley observed in the House of Lords, the Commission revealed nothing new, but drew together much that was useful. Based upon its report, the Compensation to Tenants (Ireland) Bill was introduced in the House of Lords by Stanley in June 1845. It required landlords to compensate tenants for their improvements in building, fencing, and draining should they be ejected before gathering the fruits of their improvement. In addition, a salaried Commissioner of Improvements, resident in Dublin, would supervise tenant applications for improvements. The Commissioner would maintain a registry of estates enabling him to determine whether proposed improvements would be feasible. If a landlord objected to any proposed improvements, an Assistant Commissioner, with discretionary power, would examine the estate before a final decision was reached.

Reaction to the proposal was instantly unfavourable. On 27 June 1845 *The Times* condemned it as 'mischievous and bungling' because of the complicated machinery involving the Commissioner, landlords, and tenants. In the House of Lords, opposition was even more hostile. The bill was viewed as an unacceptable violation of property rights, and united in opposition to it were such different men as the Conservative Earl of Roden, a Grand Master of the Orange Lodge; and Lord Clanricarde, an Irish Whig peer who usually took a liberal line on Irish affairs. The peers were especially incensed at the threatened intrusion of the Commissioners upon their estates: the Marquess of Londonderry declaimed against the 'junto' of the Commissioners; Lord Monteagle warned of 'despotism'.[30] Although the second reading of the bill passed, it was obvious that support for it was weak. In mid-July, Peel withdrew the bill. It is not unlikely that there was some reluctance on the part of the ministry to infringe on a landlord's prerogative to eject his tenantry when he chose. Perhaps, too, the ministry felt that the impending Maynooth question, which could no longer be postponed, was more important—too important for any diversion.

Maynooth dominated the parliamentary session of 1845. The fiercest opposition was not to the proposed increase in the grant, but to the intention of changing it from a yearly measure of grace and favour. To rabid Anglicans, this implied a revision of the existing relations between church and state and an abandonment of the Erastian principle as established at the Reformation. The Dissenting 'Voluntaries' disliked the bill because they opposed all religious establishments. This laid the basis for cooperation between Anglicans and Dissenters in the Anti-Maynooth Committee, a powerful extra-parliamentary pressure group. Also opposed to Maynooth were those Conservatives within the party who were exasperated by Peel's betrayal of implicit party pledges. He had already tampered with the Corn Laws: now he threatened the dominance of the Church of England in Ireland. The atmosphere was further embittered by the rising anti-Catholic sentiment in the 1840s which viewed any accommodation with popery as damnable. In short, for the opponents of Maynooth, the issue was not seen as a political skirmish in obscure theological thickets, but as a fight worthy of a pitched battle on the highest plane of principle.

Warning flags were flying early in the session. Gladstone tendered his long-anticipated resignation in January 1845. When news of this reached Ireland, Heytesbury reported to Peel rumours of extreme Protestant circles seeking to make Gladstone head of a Protestant party.[31] A concerned letter to Peel from Goulburn reported the apprehensions of his Cambridge University constituents. Even the liberal Master of Trinity had preached on the previous Guy Fawkes Day 'a *very* protestant sermon'. The Maynooth grant was generally regarded as 'putting arms into the hand of the Enemy'.[32] In the early weeks of the session, petitions and public meetings hostile to the ministry grew in number. But Peel remained firm: he was determined to 'risk the fate of the Government' on Maynooth.[33]

Peel introduced the details of the Maynooth bill to the House of Commons on 3 April 1845. In justifying the increased grant to Maynooth, he told the Commons that the buildings of the College were so decayed that it looked more like a 'deserted barrack' than a 'literary institution'.[34] He proposed a special grant of £30,000 for new buildings, putting the cost of repairs and maintenance under the Board of Works. By raising the annual grant from slightly more than £9,000 to £26,000, Peel could increase the salaries of the Principal and the professors, and double students' scholarships. In his most controversial proposal, Peel confirmed that the new grant would be a permanent endowment. Additional reforms included the incorporation of the trustees of the College, thus enabling them to receive property, and the establishment of a Board of Visitors to supervise the College on behalf of the government.

Once the details of the plan were made public, the anticipated opposition became vociferous. The tone of the opposition outside Parliament was set by a series of attacks on Peel in the leader columns of *The Times*. Charging that Peel governed 'by deception', *The Times* declared it far more important that British statesmen be trusted 'than that the Maynooth students should sleep one in a bed, and their College should not be mistaken for a barrack'. The effect of an increased grant to Maynooth was simple: 'Treble the endowment of Maynooth, and, of course, you multiply priests.'[35] Opposition in Parliament was no less fierce. The leading Protestant spokesman was the Conservative member for Oxford, Sir Robert Inglis, who declared that the proposal represented 'the endowment of the Church of Rome'.[36] Others objected to the removal of the Maynooth grant from an annual parliamentary scrutiny. As the debate progressed, curious alignments were revealed. The radical John Bright allied with the Conservative aristocrat Lord Ashley in speaking against the bill. Graham admitted to the House that 'the fire opens upon us from the front, the flank, and the rear'.[37] Peel, especially, took a beating, not least from his

own backbenchers. Colonel Sibthorp confessed that he had
lost all confidence in 'that man Sir R. Peel'.[38] The most
biting speech came from Disraeli, who called Peel 'a Conservative dictator' and accused him of 'cunning' and 'habitual
perfidy'.[39] Perhaps the gravest opposition of all was fore-
cast by the Conservative member for East Kent, J. E.
Plumptre, who warned the House that if they passed the bill,
they 'might expect the Divine Judgement upon them'.[40]

Peel placed his faith in more tangible support: he relied
upon a combination of liberal Conservatives, Whigs, and
Catholic Irish members to carry the bill. The bill passed its
third reading by a comfortable majority, but it was obvious
that without support from the opposition, Maynooth would
not have been enacted, for the third reading of the bill found
the Conservatives divided 149–148 against its passage.[41] The
more conservative agricultural wing of the party was especially distraught by the bill. C. Goring, MP for Shoreham,
declared that the agricultural interest viewed the Maynooth
grant 'with regret and alarm' and feared that the ministry
would soon sacrifice the agriculturists by repealing the
Corn Laws, just as they had sacrificed the Protestant church
in Ireland.[42] There is little doubt that Goring voiced the
sentiments of a large section of the Conservative party whose
loyalty toward their leadership was at the breaking point.
The significance of the Conservative opposition to Maynooth was not lost upon the ministry. In letters written to
Heytesbury during the crisis, Graham despairingly compared the fate of the government over Maynooth to the
Catholic relief struggle of 1829. Then, the extreme Protestant Conservatives had overthrown the Conservative government, ushering in more than a decade of Whig rule. Graham
predicted the same fate for the Peel ministry. Although
he thought the Maynooth bill would pass through Parliament
intact, he thought the Conservative party would be 'destroyed' by its passage. He castigated those who upheld
'High Tory principles' for not realising that the day of

Protestant ascendancy was over in Ireland. Of the Protestants in Ireland, Graham predicted that they 'will never
be wise in time. . . . We have risked much for them, and
as usual the return which we received is contumely, opposition and malignity.'[43]

The ministry encountered less opposition to its remaining
conciliatory measure, the improvement of Irish secular
education. Since 1833, Ireland had a system of national
education for its school-children. The system involved the
payment of state grants to any school for books and teach-
ers' salaries provided that the school did not promote
sectarianism. Religious instruction was purely voluntary.
The hope was that schools with a mixture of religious sects
might inculcate habits of toleration among their pupils.
Although the number of national schools increased from 789
in 1833 to 3,637 in 1846 with proportional increases in
enrolment, the ideal and practice of 'mixed' education
declined. Both Anglicans and Presbyterians, as the minority
sects in Ireland, felt more threatened by an integrated system of education than did Catholics. Consequently, the
Anglicans expanded their own separate educational system
outside the national system. From 1839 to 1846, the number
of Anglican schools more than doubled—from 825 to 1,899.
With less resources at their command, the Presbyterians,
especially in the north where their larger numbers could be
brought more effectively to bear, merely bent the rules gov-
erning religious instruction in the national schools.

Opposition to the national system was extensive enough
by 1841 to raise doubts among some members of Peel's
ministry as to the wisdom of its continuance. Both Stanley
and de Grey thought it had failed. Peel disagreed, and
impressed upon de Grey the necessity of appointing to
positions of responsibility only those who supported national education. But in this, as in other matters, de Grey
went his own way. Heytesbury, de Grey's successor, later
commented on the unfortunate tendency of de Grey's

appointments (whether bishops, deans, or chaplains to the
Lord Lieutenant) to oppose the national system.[44] Nevertheless, Peel's affirmation of national education assured its continuance.

To provide more opportunities for higher education in
Ireland, the ministry expanded the college system. In May
1845, Graham introduced the Irish Colleges Bill which established three new colleges at Cork, Galway, and Belfast. In
accordance with the aim of national education, the colleges
would be free of all religious tests and in none would there
be a faculty of theology, although private endowments for
religious instruction would be encouraged. There was little
parliamentary opposition to the bill with the exception of
Sir Robert Inglis, who condemned it as 'a gigantic scheme
of Godless education'.[45] There was more opposition to
the measure in Ireland. O'Connell and the extreme Catholics wanted separate sectarian colleges; and the Catholic
prelates hoped to make the bill more favourable to Catholic interests by, for example, ensuring that Catholic professors were appointed to chairs in sensitive subjects such as
history and metaphysics. Although Peel realised that the
northern college at Belfast would effectively become a Pres-
byterian college, and the two southern colleges become
Catholic (with Trinity College retaining its predominantly
Anglican character), he was unwilling to make them wholly
sectarian. Nor could he agree with the exclusivist requests
of the prelacy that an assured number of Catholic faculty
be appointed. Some of the more pragmatic of the hierarchy
prevailed and agreement was reached to cooperate with
the ministry in the establishment of the colleges. The bill
received the royal assent on 31 July 1845.

From this discussion of the ministry's Irish policy, it is
clear that Irish events had shifted it decisively. Neglected at
first, Ireland gradually became the ministry's most absorb-
ing concern. Peel's determined attempts at conciliation,
however belated, involved him in an ever-deepening commit-

ment to satisfy Irish grievances. When the failure of the Irish potato crop in late 1845 threatened to destroy the fragile Irish economy and subvert the policy of conciliation, Peel acted decisively, regardless of the political cost. Thus his concern for the conciliation of Ireland led him to acts that destroyed his ministry. Gladstone foretold only too accurately the fatal importance of Ireland to the ministry when he wrote in 1845: 'Ireland, Ireland! that cloud in the west, that coming storm, the minister of God's retribution upon cruel and inveterate and but half-atoned injustice!'[46]

4 RELUCTANT IMPERIALISTS

The proximity of Ireland and its problems forced upon Peel, as upon previous administrations, an active imperial policy toward that country. Ireland was, strategically speaking, too close to England for any but English interests to dominate. By contrast, the ministry hoped to follow a more relaxed policy toward other imperial possessions. This was an attitude that the ministry hoped to extend to its foreign policy as a whole, a policy it saw in traditional terms. The aims of the ministry's foreign policy included a commitment to the abolition of the international slave trade, the protection and extension of British commerce, the maintenance of British prestige abroad, and the support of the empire. Although the ministry's foreign policy was traditional in its aims, the execution of that policy marked a sharp contrast with the previous Whig administration. There were no public declarations of Britain's grand designs or blustering attempts to intimidate. Caution, deliberation, and conciliation were more characteristic of the Peel ministry's diplomatic style. However, the ministry was not always successful in the pursuit of its aims.

Britain's attempt to abolish the slave trade had long been a source of contention among the great powers. Britain had become the foremost anti-slavery nation when it abolished the slave trade in its possessions in 1807. Impelled by a vigorous anti-slavery lobby in the years that followed, Britain initiated right-of-search treaties on ships at sea. These treaties allowed right of capture where slaves or slave equipment were found on board. It usually fell to the Royal Navy to enforce them. The effort was not inconsiderable: in the 1840s, the African Squadron alone constituted one-sixth of the Royal Navy and cost £750,000 annually.[1] The ministry's attempt to extend the anti-slave-trade treaties received a favourable response only from Portugal. The ministry met a hostile reaction from the two countries that mattered, France and the United States. To these growing naval powers, Britain's insistence on controlling the trade in contraband slaves on the high seas was unacceptable: the Royal Navy, because of its greater size, would do most of the searching, as it had always done. Such treaties were regarded as nothing more than a ruse by which Britain would police the seas for her own interests. The United States was particularly hostile to Britain's anti-slavery efforts. France had at least negotiated an ineffectual treaty in the 1830s, but the United States seemed uninterested in negotiating any form of right-of-search treaty. Perhaps the American recalcitrance was not surprising in view of the slave culture of the southern states.

By the 1840s, increasing numbers of illicit slaving vessels flew the flag of the United States as a protective device. In an attempt to force the United States into an accommodation, Britain claimed a distinction between the right of visit and the right of search, the former merely an examination of a ship's papers to determine its nationality, the latter a thorough inspection of a ship's cargo. Britain also proclaimed the right of visit as a principle of international law: if it were recognised as such, the Royal Navy could act against the ships of any nation regardless of treaty. The Americans did not acknowledge the distinction between the right of visit and right of search. Indeed, the difference between the two was small. Examination of an intercepted vessel's papers could easily be extended into a search of its cargo by an over-zealous commander. Peel, who upheld the right of visit, was well aware of its potential abuse and the serious consequences that might follow. Shortly after coming to office, he instructed Aberdeen to write to the Admiralty 'without delay'. He suggested that clarifications should be made on all Royal Navy orders with respect to right of visit, and that every effort should be made 'to narrow as far as possible the grounds for American complaint'.[2] In spite of Peel's conciliatory attitude, the issue remained unsettled until 1862, when a mutual agreement between the two countries was signed.

The Peel ministry also encountered difficulties in attempting to promote commerce. Since the time of Huskisson, various ministries had negotiated bilateral commercial treaties reducing tariffs between the contracting countries. By the 1840s, however, there was an increase in protectionist sentiment that was virtually world-wide. Many countries were more interested in increasing their tariffs than in reducing them. France, for example, increased duties against British linens in 1842. In the same year, the United States imposed duties of up to 50 percent on British goods. A second reason for the ministry's lack of success in commercial negotiations was of its own making: it tended to adopt such rigid negotiating positions that potentially satisfactory agreements were occasionally prevented. Brazil provides an instructive example.

It would seem that Britain and Brazil were ideally suited for mutual trade advantages. Brazil was a new country in need of the manufactured products, especially cotton textiles, that Britain could supply. Indeed, by the late 1820s Brazil was the third largest market, behind the United States and Germany, for British goods. Britain, in turn, needed Brazilian coffee and sugar in great quantities. In 1827 a commercial treaty was concluded. By its terms, Brazil imposed no more than a 15 percent import duty on British goods and was to co-operate in abolishing the thriving slave trade off the Brazilian coast. Anglo-Brazilian Courts of Mixed Commission were established to enforce the anti-slavery clauses. In return for these concessions, the British gave little

more than recognition of the new Brazilian state. Brazil felt
the unfavourable terms of the treaty in the following years.
The limited duties on British imports (extended to other
countries by most-favoured-nation clauses) crippled Brazilian revenues. Slavery posed an additional problem. Because Brazilian landowners clung to slavery as the only
solution to a growing labour shortage, their coffee and sugar
were excluded from the British domestic market. Lacking
the active co-operation of the Brazilians, Britain assumed an
increasingly unilateral role in implementing the anti-slavery
terms of the 1827 treaty. The Brazilians regarded such
actions as an infringement of their sovereignty. As the date
of the treaty's expiration approached, Brazil was in no mood
to negotiate another.

The Peel ministry, on the other hand, was eager for
increased sugar supplies. To that end, a special mission was
sent to Brazil in 1842. Each side remained adamant, however. Britain insisted on stronger anti-slavery measures and
Brazil insisted on access to the British market for all her
goods. Peel reported to the House of Commons in April
1843 that negotiations were at a standstill. When the treaty
of 1827 expired the following year, the Brazilians allowed it
to lapse. In an effort to bring Brazil to terms, Lord Aberdeen introduced a bill in the House of Lords that strengthened restrictions against the slave trade in Brazil. The Aberdeen Act, passed in August 1845, replaced the Mixed
Commissions of the treaty of 1827 with British Courts
of Admiralty. The threat to Brazil was more than implicit.
If Brazil did not co-operate in abolishing the slave trade,
Aberdeen declared, 'it would remain for Her Majesty alone,
and by Her own means' to take appropriate action.[3] During
the remainder of the Peel ministry, some fifteen slavers
flying the Brazilian flag were taken by British cruisers and
submitted to the Admiralty Courts for adjudication. Britain
offered to repeal the Act if Brazil would agree to a co-
operative venture in abolishing the slave trade. But Brazil

was as firmly in favour of slavery as Britain was against it.

Instead of securing trading advantages for Britain, the government's policy in the case of Brazil only increased hostility between the two countries. The foreign policy aims of the ministry neatly cancelled one another out: its slave trade policy prevented the import of cheap sugar. The ministry was painfully aware of the contradiction. As Aberdeen complained to Peel: 'We are terribly hampered by this slave trade, the questions connected with which meet us in every quarter, and estrange us from our best friends.'[4] Aberdeen thought nevertheless that the ministry ought not to relax its efforts against the slave trade, and he encouraged their continuance.

Estrangement from Brazil could be viewed by the Peel ministry with a certain equanimity, but this was obviously not true with a country such as France whose greater resources and ambitions posed a substantial threat to Britain. Anglo-French relations had reached a nadir under the previous Whig administration. The displacement of the bellicose Palmerston by Aberdeen at the Foreign Office provided the opportunity for a *rapprochement*. Aberdeen's pro-French views were well known. It was he was coined the phrase 'entente cordiale' in 1844 to signify the aim of his policy. Most of the cabinet, however, did not share his views. Peel, in particular, readily took offence at the French, with Graham and Wellington closely seconding. For their part, the French seemed willing to risk conflict with Britain as they actively pushed their commerce, established naval stations and colonies where possible, and extended their influence on the Continent.

French continental policy was especially dangerous to Britain, for it threatened the European balance of power. The extension of French influence on the Continent was based upon a dynastic marriage policy which would lead to a three-power Bourbon league with centres in Paris, Madrid, and Naples. The key to the policy was the success

of a French candidate in gaining the hand of Queen Isabella
of Spain. Should Isabella, whose great-uncle was Louis-
Philippe, King of the French, be persuaded to marry a
Neapolitan prince, then the Bourbon ring would be closed.
The genealogical complexities of the scheme may be inferred
from the fact that one of the French candidates, the Comte
de Trapani, was both cousin and uncle to Queen Isabella.

British policy toward the Spanish marriage question was
officially neutral. Aberdeen publicly declared that it was a
matter for the Spanish to settle. Privately, however, the
cabinet was concerned that the French wished to follow, in
the words of Peel, 'the policy of Louis the 14th with regard
to Spain'.[5] The affair dragged on with one candidate after
another considered and discarded. Rumours reached Britain
that the French had designs on Queen Isabella's younger
sister as well. The reported intention was to marry one of
Louis-Philippe's younger sons to the Infanta. Eventually this
in fact was done, though only after the fall of Peel's ministry.
In October 1846, Queen Isabella married the reputedly im-
potent Duke of Cadiz, and the Infanta married the Duc de
Montpensier. The double marriage seemed a triumph for
French policy, but events proved it a short-lived one when
the Revolution of 1848 blasted French dynastic hopes.

Against the background of British suspicions of French
motives in Spain, a series of events occurring in the South
Pacific and the Mediterranean was to lead in 1844 to the
most serious confrontation between France and Britain
since the time of Napoleon. The conflict originated in French
attempts to regain a lost colonial empire. The islands of the
Pacific seemed especially attractive to the French. In 1839 a
company was formed in Nantes for the purpose of founding
a French colony in New Zealand, an undertaking supported
by the government. The French were, however, too late: they
were edged out (but only just) by the British New Zealand
Company. France made another attempt to establish her
presence in the Pacific in 1841, when a naval squadron

under the command of Admiral Dupetit-Thouars took possession of the Marquesas Islands. The Admiral then decided on his own responsibility to declare a protectorate over Tahiti.

The ministry could not object to French influence over Tahiti. Successive British governments had refused to bring the islands of the South Pacific within the protection of the empire, although Britain had enjoyed primacy there since the voyages of Captain Cook. The Peel ministry followed this established policy. Both Aberdeen and Peel were opposed to the occupation of Pacific stations. But the policy of British non-intervention in the Pacific islands was threatened by the manner in which Admiral Dupetit-Thouars set about his task. He established less than an amicable diplomatic precedent when he first weighed anchor off Tahiti in August 1842. He demanded from Queen Pomare reparation for the alleged ill-treatment of two French priests, and threatened a bombardment unless it was met within forty-eight hours. Since neither reparations nor resistance were possible, the Queen (advised by the French consul) requested that Tahiti be placed under French protection. These events occurred in the absence of the British consul, George Pritchard, a former Methodist missionary. When Pritchard returned to Tahiti, he regained influence over the fickle Queen Pomare and persuaded her to request British military aid. The French reacted firmly: in November 1843, Queen Pomare was deposed, French troops landed, and Tahiti was annexed outright. Pritchard, however, was undaunted. He protested to the Admiral and invited the deposed Queen to take up lodgings in his own house. Pritchard's continued defiance eventually goaded a minor French official, in the absence of the island's governor, to arrest him in March 1844. Upon the governor's return, Pritchard was released and banished from Tahiti.

News of these events had been reaching England at intervals since early 1844. Pritchard's arrival in London in July

1844 with the story of his imprisonment and expulsion was the signal for a public display of anger at the French. Militant evangelical opinion was especially outraged at the actions of Catholic France. Doubtless there were many others who felt that Tahiti ought by right to be British—or at least not French. In the House of Commons, Peel was forced to admit that Pritchard's treatment was 'a gross outrage, accompanied with gross indignity'.[6]

Had the events in Tahiti been isolated ones, Peel and his colleagues would have been less concerned. The actions of over-zealous officers could, for diplomatic reasons, be explained away. There were other incidents in mid-1844, however, which seemed to indicate that the French government had opened a calculated diplomatic offensive against Britain. In May 1844, the sailor son of Louis-Philippe, the Prince de Joinville, published a pamphlet entitled *Notes sur l'etat des forces navales de la France*. In it, the Prince discussed the possibility of war with Britain, as well as the means of strengthening the French navy. As this came from such a source, it was not surprising that the British government thought that it represented official opinion, although this proved not to be the case.

More disturbing was the growing evidence that the French were considering strong measures against Morocco. One of the chief aims of British diplomacy was to prevent Morocco from domination by European powers, for its location at the entrance to the Mediterranean gave it a strategic importance equal to Gibraltar. Growing French hegemony in neighbouring Algeria had brought a warning from Britain against any expansion of French influence in the direction of Morocco. France was undeterred, however. Border skirmishes between French Algeria and Morocco gave France a justification for intervention, and in June 1844 a squadron entered Moroccan waters under the command of no less a personage than the Prince de Joinville, fresh from the labours of authorship. In spite of diplomatic warnings by the British, within two months Tangier was bombarded.

For Peel it was the last straw. To the Duke of Wellington he wrote: 'we must not allow Louis-Philippe to establish a character at our expense. The only way to prevent this is to convince him that we are in earnest and that we are prepared for a naval war.' His message to Aberdeen was similar: 'We must look to the security of Gibraltar and of our possessions in the Mediterranean, and we cannot permit *such an exercise* of the extreme rights of war. . . .' The cabinet was united behind Peel. Graham thought that a naval war between France and England was 'inevitable' unless the quarrel between France and Morocco was speedily resolved. Even Aberdeen acquiesced, believing that 'energetick' action by Britain might soon be necessary.[7] In the face of firm diplomatic protests from Britain, the French retreated. They offered a settlement of the Pritchard affair as well as a peace treaty with Morocco. By September 1844 the crisis was over.

Hostility to France in Britain was not easily dissipated, however, and did much to influence the government's discussion of military policy in the parliamentary session of 1845. The budget-conscious Peel ministry had only grudgingly allowed military expenses in its first years. But the French crisis of 1844 overturned this careful balance between parsimony and military necessity by revealing hitherto unnoticed naval deficiencies.[8] It was discovered that coastal defences had deteriorated considerably since Napoleon's time. In addition, it was discovered that Britain had only seven serviceable ships of the line in the summer of 1844. There was also anxiety about the effect of steam power on Britain's navy. De Joinville's famous pamphlet had suggested that if the French adopted steam vessels, her navy could soon match Britain's. Powered by steam, the French navy could carry a substantial force across the Channel in defiance of wind and tide, and fall with devastating effect upon any chosen spot. The revelation of these weaknesses galvanised Peel. From the latter half of 1844 he became an ardent advocate of naval armament. His letters clearly indicate that he believed Britain to be in a state of emergency. He sought information from every relevant source, jogged his ministers into more rapid responses, and urged action where he thought it necessary. Gradually the programme took shape. More than a million pounds was added to the budget of 1845 to build new maritime bases, to strengthen the defences of existing ones, and to convert ships of the line to screw propellers and to improve their armaments. Some thought was also given to the construction of more capital ships.

The armament programme had the support of the cabinet with one important exception. It was obvious that naval rearmament would mainly be directed at France, and for this reason Aberdeen strongly opposed it. 'There is no more false maxim as applied to great states,' Aberdeen wrote to Peel, 'than that we ought to prepare for war, in order to preserve peace.'[9] Aberdeen admitted that France had for some time been making great exertions to improve her navy, but he declared there was no evidence that they were directed against Britain. Aberdeen's protestations had little effect and the disagreement festered within the cabinet throughout 1845. On 18 September 1845, Aberdeen submitted his resignation. In his resignation letter, he charged that a previous policy of friendship towards France had changed into one 'of hostility and distrust'. He further charged that the government was acting 'under the influence of panic'. Aberdeen suggested that reasons of health might be put out as the cause of his resignation.

Aberdeen's resignation was unacceptable to Peel. As he pointed out in his reply, the real reason for Aberdeen's resignation would have been all too clear to the public, and its effect on Anglo-French relations could have been the opposite to what Aberdeen wished. Under pressure from Peel, Aberdeen retracted his resignation. A promise from Wellington and Graham to moderate their anti-French feeling also contributed to Aberdeen's reconsideration. Although cabinet hostility to France was only blunted, there seems to be little doubt that Aberdeen's attitude helped promote a better diplomatic climate between France and England.

Relations with the United States were, throughout Peel's administration, no less strained than with France. Two major differences prevented amicable relations between the two countries and sharpened an historical enmity. One was the controversy over the right of search discussed above. The second was potentially more dangerous, for it concerned boundary disputes along the volatile Canadian-United States frontier. It is often forgotten that friendly relations along that frontier came about only in the 1870s: until then American covetousness of Canada was a standing threat to peace. Perhaps the most severe test of American-Canadian relations occurred in the decade following the Canadian rebellion of 1837. An active American sympathy for the rebels led to several border incidents. The most notable of these was the *Caroline* affair in which the Canadian militia burned the American vessel *Caroline*, reportedly carrying arms to the rebels: the Americans retaliated by burning a British steamboat, the *Sir Robert Peel*. In November 1840, Alexander McLeod, a British citizen, was arrested in New York on the capital charges of murder and arson in connection with the *Caroline* affair. In February 1841, Henry Stephen Fox, British minister in Washington, received instructions from Lord Palmerston that if McLeod were found guilty and executed, Fox was to quit Washington. Apparently both Fox and Lieutenant-General Sir Richard Downes Jackson, commander-in-chief in Canada, believed that Fox's departure was tantamount to war, and Jackson made preparations for such an event.[10] War was averted by the replacement of the antagonistic Whigs by the more pacific Peel ministry. The new administration adopted a cautious approach toward the United States. In September 1841, the cabinet forbade Canadian authorities from taking action against the United

States without explicit orders from London. The crisis was further eased by the acquittal of McLeod in October 1841.

Border tension remained high, however, especially along the Maine–New Brunswick frontier where boundary lines had been unsettled since 1783. Both Canada and the United States claimed territory of more than seven million acres. Tension was further heightened when the British decided to construct a road from Montreal and Quebec through the disputed territory to the military base at Halifax. To settle this issue and all other outstanding differences with the United States was an early hope of Peel's administration. In April 1842, the ministry sent Lord Ashburton as special envoy to Washington with plenipotentiary powers. The choice of Ashburton signalled Britain's friendly intentions. Ashburton was well acquainted with the United States. He was married to a Philadelphia heiress, Anne Brigham, and had extensive contacts in America through his firm, Baring and Company. Furthermore, Ashburton knew and liked his negotiating counterpart, Daniel Webster, the American Secretary of State. Ashburton's American proclivities were tested severely during several months of negotiation. He found himself in discussions not only with Webster but with the more recalcitrant representatives of the state of Maine as well. An unexpected difficulty also arose in the cabinet. Wellington was very firm for securing the whole of the disputed territory, and at first influenced Aberdeen by his determination. Aberdeen's willingness later to settle for less territory eventually made the treaty possible. The treaty, as signed in August 1842, gave approximately 4½ million acres to the United States and slightly more than 3 million to Britain, enough for the projected military road.

Like most compromises, the treaty had a mixed reception. Those who favoured it did so unenthusiastically. *The Times* typified this attitude when it declared that Ashburton had extricated Britain 'as well as could have been expected' from 'a scrape'.[11] But there were grounds for criticism in the

limited scope of the treaty. Nothing had been said of the
growing boundary dispute in the Oregon territory to the
far west. Nor had there been a settlement of the right-of-
visit dispute. These omissions provided an opportunity
which Lord Palmerston eagerly seized. During a three-hour
speech in the House of Commons in March 1843, he charged
that the negotiations had been 'ill conducted' and that the
treaty was clearly 'disadvantageous' to British interests.[12]
In private, Palmerston was even more critical. To Lord John
Russell, he castigated the treaty as 'one of the worst and most
disgraceful' ever concluded by Britain, and urged Russell to
lead the party against its acceptance.[13] Apart from mild
ciriticism of the treaty in the House of Commons, however,
Lord John did not act on Palmerston's suggestion. Few
Whigs shared Palmerston's bellicose sentiments: most
welcomed the treaty as a first step toward reducing Anglo-
American tension.

The hope of better relations between Britain and the
United States proved short-lived. By early 1844, the cabinet
was receiving reports that the Americans had launched a
powerful iron steamer on Lake Erie and were building
another on Lake Ontario. The completed vessel was the side-
wheel *Michigan*, the first iron ship of the United States Navy.
It was not clear to the cabinet whether the Rush–Bagot
agreement of 1817—which limited naval arms on the Great
Lakes—applied to steam vessels. But in any case, the American action seemed 'unfriendly' to Stanley, and, as he wrote
to Peel, could 'hardly be considered consistent with the spirit
at least of the agreement'.[14] Peel concurred. In his reply to
Stanley, he declared that unless a satisfactory response were
received from the United States, there was 'no alternative
. . . except counter-armament'.[15] The Americans claimed
that, in fact, the Rush–Bagot agreement did not apply.

The British response to continued American pressure
along the Canadian frontier was to challenge American
security on the periphery of her growing empire. British

policy toward both Texas and California may be seen in that light. Texas had been an object of American expansionists since its self-proclaimed independence from Mexico in 1836, but it had been rebuffed in its first annexation attempts by the northern states, who objected to its slave culture. Texas thus became an independent republic. Britain supported Texan independence for several reasons. Not only might Texas serve as a buffer between the American empire and British interests in Mexico and southward, but later bargaining with Texas might create a large free-trade area that would counter the protective tariffs of the United States. Humanitarian motives may even have been at work—the desire to reclaim Texas from its slavery. In 1844, therefore, Lord Aberdeen conceived a scheme in concert with France by which Mexico, still technically at war with Texas, would accept Texan independence in return for an Anglo-French guarantee of Mexican territory. Texan independence would thus be assured under British sponsorship. The venture never went far, however, and by the last half of 1844 it had failed. Mexico would not recognise Texas; Anglo-French relations were cooling; and, perhaps more important, Aberdeen realised the inevitable—that Texas must eventually become part of the United States. The election in November 1844 of James K. Polk as the President of the United States on an expansionist programme made the annexation of Texas only a matter of time, and indeed, the following year Texas was received into the Union.

Aberdeen's abortive Mexican policy merely had the effect of raising suspicions against Britain among the American expansionists. The expansionists believed that America was destined to become a transcontinental empire, as the annexation of Texas had manifestly indicated. Texas had opened the way to the far west: only California and Oregon remained to complete the expansionist dream. But there were fears that Britain had designs on both territories. California, a province weakly held by Mexico, seemed especially vulner-

able. California could become the key to British encircle-
ment of the United States, including Canada to the north,
Mexico as an ally to the south, and the West Indies farther
to the east. American fears were not entirely unfounded.
British agents in California throughout the 1830s and 1840s
frequently advocated an increased British presence there.
Men of influence such as Sir George Simpson, the governor
of the Hudson's Bay Company, were also eager for Califor-
nian territory. More important, there was some cabinet
interest in California. In a letter to Peel dated 23 September
1845, Aberdeen reported a conversation just concluded with
the Mexican minister. The minister had indicated his belief
to Aberdeen that war between the United States and Mexico
was imminent. In such an event, Mexican defence of California would be impossible. Would Britain, in collabora-
tion with Mexico, protect California from an invasion by
the United States? There was no reason why Britain should
not aid a soveriegn nation against the threatened incursions
of an aggressor. Furthermore, it provided another opportunity for Anglo-French co-operation. As Aberdeen put it to
Peel: 'if we could succeed in enlisting France for her own
interests, cordially to unite in resisting American aggression,
it would be a great stroke of policy. . . .'[16] French co-operation was perhaps not an unreasonable assumption, given
growing French interest in the Pacific. There was no thought
of procuring California as a British colony, although the
scheme would deny California to the Americans. Peel, however, quashed the California scheme. He thought the plan
came too late, and that *bona fide* British interests were not
well enough established there to justify it.[17]

Although conflict between the United States and Britain
over California was thus averted, another crisis in the
Oregon territory soon threatened a rupture in Anglo-
American relations. The western boundary between the
United States and Canada had been unsettled for decades,
as had been their eastern boundary. The issue had been

dormant until large numbers of American settlers moved into Oregon in the early 1840s. As American interest in Oregon grew, demands for its annexation rose proportionately. Polk's election to the presidency in 1844 brought a climax to the excitement over Oregon. One of Polk's more famous campaign slogans—'Fifty-four forty or fight'—was taken as a pledge to annex to that northern latitude. Britain could not allow the American claim, for the Hudson's Bay Company held trading posts as far south as the Columbia river near the forty-sixth parallel.

Throughout 1845 Polk's public statements did not suggest that an amicable settlement was possible; his inaugural address, in March 1845, threatened force in Oregon. This intransigence united Whigs and Conservatives in Parliament against the United States. Lord John Russell denounced the 'arrogant pretensions' of the Americans, and Peel made it plain that Britain had 'clear and unquestionable rights in Oregon'.[18] Aberdeen echoed his chief in the House of Lords, warning that 'there are limits which must not be passed. . . .'[19]

For the first time since 1841 there was a prospect of war with the United States. The cabinet set about devising a strategic policy. There was never any doubt in the minds of the cabinet members—with the inevitable exception of the Duke of Wellington—that the policy must be a defensive one. Britain's most potent offensive weapon, her naval power, could only be brought to bear in a limited way on the land mass of the United States. Nor could an overextended imperial army be effectively utilised without great cost. A more economical military force, the Canadian militia, was relatively small and inefficient when compared with the American militia. The cabinet decided to create a more effective militia, to shore up defensive sites, and to determine which steam vessels on the Great Lakes might be most readily convertible to military use.

Even as Anglo-American relations worsened, however, there

were forces for compromise. It was clear to Peel and his colleagues that the increasing numbers of American settlers must in time make Oregon *de facto* American. Nor was there much of value for Britain in the territory: even the Hudson's Bay Company fur trade was declining. Britain was willing, therefore, to accept the forty-ninth parallel as a compromise boundary provided that the Hudson's Bay Company's property was respected south of that line. American willingness to compromise was based partly on a growing realisation among commercial men that everything of maritime value, especially good harbours, lay south of the forty-ninth parallel. Perhaps a more important influence on the American position was their knowledge of Britain's strengthened naval forces. The United States was unprepared for war. American weakness in naval steamships was especially marked: they had only 7, mounting 39 guns, compared to the British total of 141, mounting 698 guns. During the last stage of the Oregon negotiations, Britain pressed its advantage. In February 1846, Aberdeen held a stiff interview with the American minister, Louis McLane. Aberdeen's warning that British patience was wearing thin was transmitted to Washington. Historians debate the importance of this interview in promoting the final compromise, but it seems likely that increased British truculence predisposed the Americans to agreement. The outbreak of the American war with Mexico in May 1846 was a further incentive to compromise. The only remaining obstacle lay with President Polk, whose speeches left him little room for manoeuvre. In June 1846, however, he announced that a compromise submitted by the British Foreign Office would be first sent to the Senate for its advice. This reversal of customary procedure allowed Polk to be persuaded by the Senate (which he knew favoured the compromise) to accept the treaty. Face was saved and the treaty was signed on 15 June 1846, making the forty-ninth parallel the permanent boundary. Although controversy over Oregon was not stilled until 1872, when arbitration settled the final details, it no longer threatened the peace along the Canadian border.

The ministry had avoided conflict in Europe and America by exercising an effective diplomacy. The same cannot be said of its policy toward other nations. War in Asia, for example, was endemic during the whole of the Victorian era and the 1840s were no exception. Peel's administration not only inherited wars in China and India, but also fought and concluded two other short wars in India. These conflicts added Hong Kong and Scinde to the empire, and prepared the way for the addition of the Punjab. By less violent means, Natal and the island of Labuan, off Borneo, were annexed. The exercise of British power did not always bring rewards, however. There was an unsuccessful military intervention in Latin America, which was an embarrassing episode for the ministry.

It is obvious that during the Peel ministry Britain was engaged in imperialism as much as during the more celebrated imperial administrations later in the century. Yet the cabinet itself was not the force behind imperial expansion. Peel, Aberdeen, Stanley, and Gladstone all opposed an extension of the empire. Unknown costs and diplomatic dangers cooled their imperial ardour. Peel even confessed his disillusion with the existing 'onerous' colonial burden and seemed, in moments of pique, not unwilling to let some of the colonies go their own way.[20] Yet, in spite of the ministry's reluctance to add to the burden of empire, imperial additions were made. How can this paradox be explained? There were two major motivations for imperial expansion during the 1840s—the strategic and the commercial. The ministry felt compelled to annex on strategic grounds when any part of the empire was threatened by unfriendly forces or potential invaders: in such cases, territories contiguous to imperial lands were taken as buffer zones. Natal, for example, was annexed in 1842 with the intention of improving the security of the Cape Colony against the warring Boer and

Zulu. The major impetus for imperial expansion in the 1840s, however, was commercial rather than strategic.

Commercial entrepreneurs, seeking wider markets, exerted continuous pressure on governments to extend trade by treaty if possible, by force if necessary. Traders were not backward in taking matters into their own hands. Their bumptious adventurism was an embarrassment to the government and an intrusion on high policy. But the government's commitment to trade expansion and the protection of British interests drew them inevitably into commercial hostilities and ultimately war with other countries.

China provided the clearest example of the formidable international power of British commerce. China's reluctance to open her vast potential market was a long-standing grievance to British traders. Not only had the Chinese imposed severe restrictions on trade, but they had restricted the movement and residence of foreigners within China as well. Although it seems that traditional Chinese distaste for commerce played some role in its indifference to foreign trade, it was also true that agrarian China was largely self-sufficient. On the other hand, China had one commodity of surpassing interest to the British—tea. As British tea consumption increased in the nineteenth century, the trade gap between China and Britain widened. To redress the balance, British merchants increased exports of the two staples that had a market in China, raw cotton and opium. Both products could be supplied from British India.

British opium exports to China were profitable: opium had 'the small bulk, imperishability, steady demand, and wide market most to be desired in a product'.[21] It soon became more important than cotton in the China market. In the decade before 1842, opium constituted about two-thirds of the value of all British exports to China, increasing from slightly over 9,000 chests in 1824 to more than 40,000 in 1839. The opium trade eventually yielded one-seventh of the total revenue of British India.[22] It was, however, an illegal trade. Chinese imperial edicts prohibited both the smoking of opium and its importation. This did not deter the traders: officials were bribed and an extensive smuggling network was organised. By the later 1830s, when opium smuggling reached its height, Chinese officials decided to take firm measures. Both sellers and smokers were seized. British traders were not impressed by this display of energy from the Chinese. Led by the notorious James Innes, they carried their cargoes up-river in armed cutters directly to smokers willing to pay high prices. Relations between the Chinese and the traders deteriorated further in March 1839, when a special imperial commissioner seized all opium in China, including some 20,000 chests of British opium worth £2,400,000.

What had originally been a conflict between British merchants and the Chinese government eventually involved the British government. In 1834, Britain had established a resident Superintendent of British Trade in China who assisted British subjects in their mercantile pursuits. When the confiscation order was issued by the Chinese in 1839, Superintendent Charles Elliott acted in defence of British citizens' property. This precipitated hostilities. The ensuing war—an affair of intermittent small-scale infantry and naval clashes—ended with the Treaty of Nanking in August 1842. The treaty opened four ports for British trade on the Chinese coast, and ceded the island of Hong Kong to Britain.

The hostilities of 1839–42, usually known as the first of the Opium Wars, settled a broader issue than the right of British merchants to peddle opium in China. The war aims of the merchants had been no less than the establishment of a commercial centre in China under the British flag, and freedom of trade throughout China. To a great extent these aims were achieved. For many contemporaries, however, the war had been a dishonourable episode. The spectacle of British power forcing open a market that would benefit

opium traders was unedifying. *The Times* was frequently
critical: it looked with 'almost unmixed pain' on a 'discreditable' war, and thought the acquisition of Hong Kong
'unjustifiable'.[23] The Peel ministry, which had inherited the
war from the Whigs, had similar reservations. Gladstone,
before joining the cabinet, sought assurances that the
ministry would not compensate the merchants for their
confiscated opium.[24] Peel thought that every care should be
taken to ensure that the opium trade was conducted 'in a
manner less discreditable to us than that in which it has been
hitherto conducted'.[25]

The ministry was also somewhat unhappy with the Treaty
of Nanking. The acquisition of Hong Kong was not meant
to be permanent. The official war aims disclaimed any territorial acquisition,[26] and the island was taken early in the
war only as a bargaining counter. But it was immediately
flooded with merchants and speculators who quickly seized
the trading opportunities which Hong Kong afforded. This
was a matter of concern to the cabinet. 'The immense influx
of wealth and inhabitants,' Aberdeen wrote to Stanley,
'with the great works in progress undertaken by private persons, must create interest which it will everyday become more
difficult to abandon.' Aberdeen disliked the idea of any
permanent British settlement in China. 'The certain expense,
the nature of our relations with that strange Empire, and the
probable embarrassment it would create with other Powers,
make it desirable not to encourage such a project.'[27] Stanley was similarly inclined. In his reply to Aberdeen, he wrote
that he preferred trade with China based upon treaty, rather
than on 'the occupation of a Chinese Gibraltar or two, the
commerce of which would be in the main of an illicit character. . . .' Stanley, like Aberdeen, realised how difficult it
would be 'to abandon the large amount of property which
has been invested there. . . .'[28] In the end, however, commercial interest overrode the reservations of a reluctant cabinet, and Hong Kong remains today a British Crown Colony.

Government intervention on behalf of British commerce was not always successful. The La Plata episode in Latin America is a case in point. British trading interests were dominant from the earliest days of the newly independent countries of Latin America. Political turmoil, however, continually threatened their commercial pursuits. In the 1840s, for example, hostilities between Argentina and Uruguay jeopardised the important trading route of the river Plate, which divided the two states. British sympathy was alienated from Argentina by the harshness of the regime of General Rosas, a cattle owner whose life had been spent among the gauchos of the Pampas. Rosas was not schooled in the niceties of free trade or even persuaded of the value of trade.

At first Aberdeen was reluctant to interfere in such a remote controversy. In 1841, he had turned down a Foreign Office memorandum suggesting a system of countervailing alliances in South America for the purpose of maintaining a peaceful equilibrium in the interests of trade. It proved difficult to remain aloof, however, in the face of Rosas' intransigence and the Uruguayan sympathies of British officials in Latin America. Furthermore, the ministry was under pressure from British merchants, who wanted better protection for their trade in Latin America. By late 1844, Aberdeen's views had changed. He envisaged a joint action by France and Britain which could quickly bring about a settlement. Such a policy would not only satisfy commercial circles, but would promote closer relations with France. After some urging by Aberdeen, France agreed.

What precise action Aberdeen had in mind is unclear. In a letter dated 8 October 1845 to William Gore Ouseley, British minister at Buenos Aires, Aberdeen's tone was warlike. He acknowledged the necessity of coercive actions, and expressed the hope that they would be executed 'with vigour'.[29] Two months later, Aberdeen had second thoughts and urged a more conciliatory course. It seems he now thought that a naval demonstration, or at most a blockade, would suffice. In the meantime, events in the Argentine had gone their own way. Ouseley, instructed to persuade Rosas to remove his troops from Uruguay, had decided on force. Utilising a British naval unit and with the co-operation of a French squadron, Ouseley ordered an armed convoy up-river. In November 1845 a sharp engagement took place between the convoy and Argentinian defensive emplacements. This intervention merely heightened Argentinian patriotism and enflamed feeling against the British. It was now obvious to Aberdeen that naval action alone would not dislodge Rosas: troops would be necessary. In December 1845, Aberdeen confessed to Peel that he had been badly misinformed by 'all the officers professing to have local knowledge' of the affairs in the Argentine.[30] He concluded gloomily: 'we have entered upon a task which it will be scarcely possible for us fully to accomplish, and from which it will not be easy to withdraw with honour'.[31] The ministry decided on disengagement, a policy continued by Palmerston after the fall of the Peel ministry in 1846. Gunboat diplomacy had been proved a failure.

The La Plata affair gave point to cabinet reluctance to become involved in the support of British commercial claims. Foreign entanglements could mean over-extension, thus endangering well-established interests elsewhere. Even when territorial acquisitions might be received into the empire virtually as gifts, the ministry did not act with enthusiasm. No better example can be cited than the establishment of the British presence in Borneo.

The opening of Borneo is associated with James Brooke, in whose career commercial adventurism reached its epitome. Born in 1803 in India where his father was employed by the East India Company, Brooke was early influenced by Sir Stamford Raffles' dream of British hegemony over the Malay States. When his father's death left him a substantial inheritance, Brooke purchased a schooner with the idea of trading in those islands of the east that had captured Raffles' imagination and his own. Soon after his arrival in Borneo he found himself involved on the side of the Sultan of Brunei in suppressing a revolt of the Sultan's subjects. The Sultan made Brooke rajah and governor of Sarawak in November 1841, as a reward for his successful intervention.

Brooke had little administrative experience and few advisers, apart from the crews of his two ships, to govern a province the size of Yorkshire. Therefore, from the first, Brooke tried to interest the British government in his exploits. In 1842, he published a pamphlet in which he urged the establishment of a strong British influence in Borneo. In January 1843, Brooke's agent in Britain, Henry Wise, had an interview with Peel, the result of which was the despatch of a surveying ship to Borneo. Ministerial interest was prompted not by colonial prospects, but by the need to protect British commerce, for several acts of piracy in nearby waters had resulted in the capture and ill-treatment of British subjects. The ministry thought a naval station in the region might prevent recurring incidents, and the discovery of coal on the small island of Labuan, off the North-western coast of Borneo, directed British attention there. Using his official position, Brooke secured the cession of Labuan to Britain in 1844.

Labuan had a low ministerial priority, however, and for nearly two years its occupation was delayed. Finally, in June 1846, prompted by internal disturbances in Borneo, Aberdeen sent an urgent letter to Gladstone, the new Colonial Secretary, requesting the immediate establishment of a naval station on Labuan. Gladstone at first refused, being fearful that a naval station would lead to permanent settlement. In his labyrinthine way, Gladstone explained his disapproval of further colonial expansion.

> The multiplication of colonies at the other end of the world must at all times be a matter of serious consideration: but especially at a time when we have already land almost infinite

to defend that we cannot occupy, people to reduce to order
whom we have not been able to keep in friendly relations, and
questions in so many departments of government to manage,
the discussion of which has been found embarrassing at
home, and which appear to be thought fully equal in the
demands they make, to any energies that the Executive Government is able to apply to them. I confess that as being
responsible for the Government of the Colonies I am struck
by the enormous field as yet unoccupied but distinctly
belonging to us which we have to fill: by the singular com-
plication which distance gives to our affairs in that quarter:
[and] by the weight of our responsibilities there already
incurred. . . .'[32]

Gladstone pointed out that he was not alone in his opinion.
The Admiralty could do their job 'without any fixed centre
of motion'; and the Treasury was flatly opposed to the scheme
since it would mean an addition of 300 men to Antipodean
forces. In short, Gladstone concluded, the subject was 'not
ripe for action'.[33]

   Gladstone's objections elicited from Aberdeen a sharp
reply.[34] He observed that 'the concurrent testimony of almost every Mercantile Association in the Kingdom, and of
every individual acquainted with the course of Trade in those
Seas' had urged a naval station between Singapore and Hong
Kong for the protection of commerce. There was reason for
urgency in that recent disturbances in Borneo could imperil
the project: Brooke himself might be endangered. Furthermore, the disturbances were regarded 'by some, as by the
Manchester Chamber of Commerce, . . . in part attributable to the lukewarmness' of the ministry in the matter.
Admitting that some permanent settlement in Labuan might
be necessary, Aberdeen contended that it would be small,
and he reassured Gladstone of the ministry's official anti-
expansionist policy. Aberdeen's letter to Gladstone was written only days before the ministry fell. It was left to the Whigs
to occupy the island.

The Labuan incident provides another example of cabinet reluctance to support colonial expansion. Neither Aberdeen nor Gladstone desired Labuan (or Borneo, for that matter) as colonies of residence. Gladstone saw perhaps more clearly that even a token presence on Labuan might assure an increased British presence in all of Borneo. As he had put it in his letter to Aberdeen, there was every likelihood that, with a colony off the coast, Britain would eventually make its way to the mainland 'so as to have relations not only with its commerce and people, but with its soil and with the dominion over it'.[35]

Cabinet reluctance to support commercial adventurism may also be seen in its colonial policy. New Zealand provides the best example. A colony since 1840, New Zealand had immediately become a theatre of conflicting aspirations, with humanitarian interests and missionary groups being pitted against the commercial developers and colonisers. The moving spirit of the colonists and commercial men was Edward Gibbon Wakefield, who had worked out his theories on systematic colonisation while serving a three-year prison sentence in Newgate for abducting a fifteen-year-old heiress. One scheme of ready wealth having failed, he had turned his energies eagerly to another. The heart of his system was the proposal that colonial lands were to be set at a high enough price—a 'sufficient price'—so that the working-class immigrant would be unable to purchase land until he had worked for some years in the colony. By this means, a proper balance between capital and labour would be established. Of course, it also meant that the organisers of any such colony would profit considerably through the subsequent rise in real estate values. It was a scheme, as one critic has noted, well worthy of a land agent's son.[36] Wakefield's scheme was lent a respectable tone by those who thought a rational plan of encouraged emigration would reduce population pressures in Britain, open up new markets, and create new opportunities for investment. Calling themselves colonial reformers, Wakefield's supporters included such notable Benthamites as John Stuart Mill, Sir William Molesworth, and Lord Durham. The most effective parliamentary voice was Charles Buller, MP for Liskeard (Cornwall).

The Colonial Office, under the influence of James Stephen, Permanent Under-Secretary, opposed Wakefield and the expansionists. Stephen, whose anti-slavery views had already made their mark on official British policy through successive administrations, feared the effect of colonial expansion upon the indigenous Maori tribesmen. Stephen's opinions were reinforced by Peel's Colonial Secretary, Lord Stanley. Stanley had a more specific complaint against the New Zealand Company, which had organised the colonisation. As Stanley confided to Peel, he was opposed to the company because of 'the pei etual small trickery which from first to last has charact rised their proceedings'.[37] Indeed, there was much that was questionable in the company's history. Wakefield had founded the company in 1839, with Lord Durham as its titular head. Its most important financial backers were the shipping magnates Joseph Somes and G. F. Young. Somes already dominated the trade with Australia and was the greatest shipowner in the City of London. John Ward, the secretary of the company, and Wakefield himself were in charge of the company's publicity. They extolled by pamphlet the virtues of New Zealand, a country which neither had seen. From offices in the Strand, the company sent out agents to more than fifty British cities. Recruiting agents received a commission of 40s for every married couple and 10s for each unmarried adult enrolled in the Company's books. It seems that on occasion agents' zeal for a commission exceeded the accuracy of their descriptions of the colony. Part of the undoubted attraction to prospective colonists was the ease by which land was distributed: it was settled by lottery in London. Most of the land sold by the Company, however, eventually fell into the hands of absentee speculators, including Wakefield, who had a stake worth £1,000 at Port Nicholson.

When the first boatload of colonists left for New Zealand in 1839, not only had the voyage not been authorised by the government, but the New Zealand Company itself was of doubtful status. To protect the natives from colonial exploitation, the Whig government (urged by Stephen at the Colonial Office) hurriedly made a treaty with fifty native chiefs in February 1840. By acknowledging the Maoris as subjects of the Crown, the treaty guaranteed them exclusive and undisputed possession of their lands. This was clearly antithetical to the lottery policy of the New Zealand Company, which sought to redistribute the land among its colonists regardless of native claims. The Treaty of Waitangi, as it was called, remained the policy of the Peel government toward New Zealand.

The ministry's pro-Maori policy outraged the company and the colonial reformers. Relations between the Colonial Office and the colonists deteriorated further when the ministry upheld Maori claims in clashes between them and company surveyors. Matters came to a head in June and July 1845 when Buller moved resolutions in the House of Commons that condemned the ministry's New Zealand policy. In arguing for a more favourable policy toward the company, Buller delcared that it was 'wicked to dispute the right of man to cultivate the wilderness'.[38] In reply, ministerial supporters agreed that private companies could colonise best, but insisted that native rights must be protected. Peel put the ministry's policy in strong terms, declaring that it would not 'undertake to dispossess, by force, and against the will of the inhabitants, the natives from certain lands desired by the New Zealand Company. . . .'[39] Nevertheless, the ministry did soften its hostility to the company. Stanley soon made more land available to the colonists by purchasing it from the Maoris. Once again, commercial interests had successfully influenced the ministry.

The most active region of imperial expansion during
Peel's ministry was on the Indian sub-continent. India
provides perhaps the clearest example of strategic and commercial considerations overcoming ministerial reluctance to
annex territory. The ministry's Indian policy was initially
dictated by the inherited warfare on the north-west frontier.
Known as the First Afghan War, it was an outgrowth of
Palmerston's attempt to check Russian influence—real or
imagined—in Afghanistan. By the time Peel's Governor-
General, Lord Ellenborough, reached India in February
1842, the war was going badly. A British-led force of
6,000 Indian troops had been massacred by the Afghans,
sixteen Englishwomen carried off by the attackers, and the
British agent, Sir William MacNaghten, decapitated. Mac-
Naghten's head—the mouth of which was stuffed with 'a
portion of his mutilated body'[40]—was paraded through
Kabul as a symbol of victory. Such grisly treatment of a
British subject demanded retribution, and Ellenborough
achieved it. By late 1842, two British armies had entered
Kabul, freed the imprisoned Englishwomen, and restored
British honour.

Peace and an enhanced reputation provided Ellenborough with the opportunity for setting in motion his own
policy. Early in his career, he had become obsessed with the
idea of opening Central Asian markets to Britain, thus fore-
stalling any Russian advance. It was a policy not unlike
Palmerston's. As President of the Board of Control in
Wellington's administration of 1828–30, Ellenborough had
sponsored with the Duke an ostensible mission of friendship
to Runjeet Singh, the Maharajah of Lahore. Disguising their
real intentions, they decided on a gift of horses to the
Maharajah. They would be sent via the Indus river, the
likely key to commercial traffic in Central Asia. The ruse
was initially successful: the horses were sent and the British
won trading concessions from the Maharajah. But later
trading ventures were unsuccessful. Restrictive tolls on the
lower Indus prevented an active trade. Ellenborough's am-

bitions in Central Asia had not dimmed through the years, however. As Governor-General of India and with a victorious army under his command, he moved in early 1843 to bring the Indus under British control. The lower reaches of the Indus flowed through Scinde, a desolate country equal in area to England and Wales, but with a population of scarcely 1¼ million in 1840. During the Afghan War, British troops had passed through Scinde, gaining the right to do so by treaty. Using the excuse that Scinde had acted in an unfriendly manner and that its rulers, the Ameers, were an alien and unpopular military clique (which was true enough), Ellenborough forced upon the Ameers a cession of territory after the war. Ellenborough also appointed to full military command in the Scinde, Sir Charles Napier, a man who believed as firmly as Ellenborough in the mission of freeing the Indus for British commerce. Within a short time, Napier had provoked an armed confrontation with one of the Ameers, and by February 1843 there was war between the Ameers and Britain. On 17 February 1843, Napier, with only 2,800 men, defeated at Miani an Ameer army estimated at between 20,000 and 30,000. When word of the victory reached Ellenborough, he immediately annexed the whole of Scinde. A few days later, he appointed Napier Governor of the new province.

Ellenborough's precipitate action caught the cabinet and the public by surprise. The reaction was largely unfavourable. Peel deplored especially the reputed mistreatment of the captured Ameers and told a cabinet meeting that Ellenborough's actions were 'unjust and indefensible'.[41] *The Times* condemned Ellenborough's policy as one of 'agression, conquest, and spoliation'.[42] As more information about Scinde reached Britain in the following months, opposition to Ellenborough grew. He became a subject of debate in Parliament where Lord John Russell condemned his 'presumptuous arrogance'.[43] There is little doubt that Ellenborough's grand schemes alarmed friend and critic alike.

Ellenborough's shortcomings were well known to his colleagues prior to his assumption of office. Even before his departure for India, there were signs of what one historian has called his 'latent megalomania'.[44] For example, he requested the commission of Captain-General and Commander-in-Chief as well as Governor-General. Since this was contrary to recent practice, Peel refused. In another bid to enhance his authority, he obtained permission from the Queen to write directly to her on matters of state. Unknown to the cabinet, Ellenborough followed this practice with every mail. The cabinet's attention was drawn to this correspondence in early 1843 when the Queen showed Peel one of Ellenborough's letters that suggested the Queen should become Empress of India. Peel rebuked Ellenborough for this unauthorised suggestion, and for his habit of circumventing the cabinet on important issues. Unrepentant, Ellenborough declared that his idea was one that he had 'very long entertained'.[45] His belief in himself as the master of India is clear enough in his unguarded moments. In a revealing letter to his sister, Anne Colville, shortly after his annexation of Scinde, he wrote: 'You see I have got a new Province, hereafter to be rich as Egypt, thrown into my lap by fortune.' Realising that his action might be severely criticised, Ellenborough nevertheless believed that the day would come 'when all England will go upon its knees to implore me to . . . save the Empire. . . .'[46]

Peel had hoped that Ellenborough, once in India, could be held in check by sound advisers. The cabinet obviously could not act as a restraining hand because of the distances involved. Cabinet responses to specific problems in India were three months in coming, the mails taking six weeks each way. On occasion, it could be longer if the mails were lost or delayed, a not uncommon occurrence. Mails might also be missed, as in 1842 when Peel was with the Queen in Scotland and lost the opportunity to respond to one of Ellenborough's letters. Distance increased Ellenborough's authority. His actions had the effect of *faits accomplis* and there was

little the cabinet could do. This was certainly true in the conquest and annexation of Scinde which took place before a
cycle of Indian and cabinet mail could have been completed.
The cabinet acquiesced in the annexation, not as a desirable
course of action, but because they had 'no other alternative'.[47]
To the ministry's way of thinking, a reversal of Ellenborough's decision would undermine his authority and could
have incalculable consequences throughout the whole of
India.

The controversy over Ellenborough did not cease with the
cabinet's sanction of his annexation of Scinde, for he had
also antagonised the East India Company by his actions.
The company, through its Court of Directors, governed
India jointly with the President of the Board of Control. In
theory, the company concerned itself with commercial matters and the Board of Control with political affairs, although
in practice this division tended to be blurred. In any case, a
Governor-General had to satisfy both the company and the
government, since either could independently recall him.
The company had been uneasy with the tendency of Indian
policy since the late days of the previous Whig administration. To an established commercial enterprise such as the
East India Company, a forward policy was undesirable. It
could mean war, the disruption of commerce, unnecessary
expense and eventually the loss of profits. Shortly after the
formation of the Peel ministry, an important memorandum
from Sir Henry Willock, Deputy Chairman of the East
India Company, expressed the company's opposition to a
forward policy. The memorandum deplored the Afghan War
as 'a fruitless enterprise' and recommended a withdrawal
from Afghanistan at the earliest possible opportunity. Sir
Henry was fearful that the war might lead to the annexation
of Afghanistan whose scarce resources 'would not cover a
fiftieth part' of the expenses needed to secure the region.
Furthermore, these 'trans Indus expenses' were delaying the
improvements in navigation and communication which the

company had planned for the far more valuable Indian empire.[48] When it dawned on the company that Ellenborough was as avid an expansionist as his Whig predecessors, they were thoroughly alarmed.

Fitzgerald, the President of the Board of Trade, spent much of his time mediating the differences between Ellenborough and the Court of Directors. After Fitzgerald's death in May 1843, Ripon, his replacement, saw the relationship between Ellenborough and the Court deteriorate further. In late 1843, Peel wrote to Wellington that some thought should soon be given to a successor to Ellenborough since it was obvious that the Court would eventually force his removal.

Peel's prediction was realised in April 1844 when the Court recalled Ellenborough. Peel was opposed to their action, for it did, after all, reflect upon the government. He even toyed with the idea of abolishing the power of the Court to recall the Governor-General, but thought it impossible 'to carry Lord Ellenborough through the House of Commons'.[49] A certain amount of face was saved when Peel replaced Ellenborough with the Secretary at War, Sir Henry Hardinge. Hardinge was Ellenborough's brother-in-law and good friend, but was more phlegmatic than his flamboyant kinsman.

Hardinge hoped to reverse the forward policy of previous Indian administrations that had led to hostilities on the north-west frontier. Within a short time, however, he was forced to make defensive preparations against the imminent threat of war with the Sikhs. The Sikhs, a reformist Hindu sect, were located in the Punjab, a great plain lying between the Indus and Sutlej rivers. During the early nineteenth century they had developed into a well-ordered state. The most dynamic section of its society was its army, a formidable force trained and disciplined on European lines. The annexation of the Scinde, cutting off the Sikh route to the sea, aroused suspicions of British intentions. Although

Hardinge was determined not to provoke the Sikhs, by November 1845 tension was mounting along the boundary of British India and the Punjab at the banks of the Sutlej. On 11 December 1845, a considerable Sikh army crossed the Sutlej. The First Sikh War had begun.

Within a few weeks four fierce battles were fought. The war went unevenly at first, but the relatively better organised British troops were successful in the end. Hardinge, as he repeatedly told Peel in his despatches, was opposed to further annexation in India. He had opposed the annexation of Scinde, believing it would be a 'dead weight'. His policy was endorsed by Peel, who thought the Indian Empire already 'overgrown'.[50] Yet the Treaty of Kasure concluding the First Sikh War annexed substantial territory. Strategic considerations had obviously overcome ministerial reluctance to add more territory to the Indian Empire.

In conclusion, it may be useful to place imperialism during Peel's administration within the context of recent scholarly debate on the nature of Victorian imperialism. There is now little doubt about the reality of early Victorian imperial expansion: there was as much between 1815 and 1870 as during the years of classic imperialism, 1870–1900. There has been a good deal of debate, however, about the precise nature of the earlier variety of Victorian imperialism. The argument has centred on the relationship between imperialism and the free-trade ideology of the era. Robinson and Gallagher maintain that free trade complemented imperialism by encouraging what they call 'informal' control.[51] This may be defined as sufficient economic influence over a client country to dictate its trading policies. Sufficient informal control would bring as great an economic return as formal annexation. Since Britain, as the leading industrial country, would benefit most if free trade were the dominant economic system, the promotion of free trade was a consistent aim of British policy. Robinson and Gallagher cite as examples the Latin

American countries, where commercial treaties formed the opening wedge of informal control. But this argument assumes too much success for official British attempts to promote trade through negotiation. Brazilian resistance to British commercial influence comes to mind. Peru also successfully resisted informal control.[52] In opposition to Robinson and Gallagher, Professor MacDonagh holds that free trade was an anti-imperial ideology.[53] This, he claims, may best be seen in the writings of Cobden, who upheld the 'natural' and pacific tendency of free trade against a coercive imperial system. But this view is unconvincing, arguing as it does from a special case. One wonders how representative Cobden's opinions were. Another argument, Professor Platt's, admits that although Victorian governments were committed to promoting trade, they were opposed to doing so by force, since this would interfere with the free market mechanism, thus violating the very canons of free trade they sought to uphold.[54] Professor Platt's is a useful corrective, but his argument probably over-estimates the role of free-trade ideology in the government's calculations.

In fact, each of these arguments encounters difficulties it could avoid by reducing the emphasis placed on free-trade ideology. It seems unlikely that British merchants were much concerned with free-trade theories, except in so far as they might justify the pursuit of profit. Cobden's insistence on the irenic nature of unhindered commerce becomes less credible in the light of the activity of the Chinese opium merchants, of Rajah Brooke in Borneo, or of the New Zealand colonists. The line between sharp commercial practice and warfare is a thin one, and it was often broached by merchants on the make. When they realised how easily the undeveloped markets could be conquered by force of arms, they were all the more encouraged. It was a time, as one historian has noted, of 'cheap glory'. Once those distant lands had 13-inch mortars at their command, however, the days of cheap glory were numbered.[55] Until then, imperial advance would continue, led by commercial men and empire builders and sanctioned by governments even when, as in Peel's case, they did so reluctantly.

5 THE END OF THE MINISTRY

Peel's main interest and energy were directed less toward foreign affairs than toward domestic. Mitigating the economic and social consequences of an industrialising nation was his first priority. But in this aim, as we have seen, he did not always carry with him the full support of his own party. Peel, who had never hidden his dislike of what he once called 'party littleness',[1] became increasingly convinced that the aims of many of his party were at odds with the needs of the country. From mid-1845, the division between Peel and his party noticeably widened, and within months became an irreparable breach.

Ironically, the issue that precipitated the crisis of confidence between the Conservative party leadership and the Conservative rank and file was not a domestic issue: it was what Peel himself once called 'that great standing evil which counterbalances all good—the state of Ireland'.[2] In the late summer of 1845, disquieting rumours of the failure of some of the Irish potato crop reached England. It was caused by a fungus hitherto unknown to scientists. The potato blight was not limited to Ireland: the whole of central and western Europe was threatened by it during the cold and wet summer of 1845, but the blight was more serious to Ireland because of that country's dependence on the potato as food for its peasantry. The significance of a poor potato crop in Ireland was realised immediately by Peel. If potatoes should completely fail in Ireland and Europe, and the wheat crop fall short in England, then famine might ensue. Peel well knew the appalling consequences of famine. As Chief Secretary to Ireland in 1817, he had witnessed an Irish famine: he had not forgotten the accompanying death and disease, and the social disorientation of a starving peasantry.

Anxious letters on the weather and the state of the potato crop passed between Peel and Graham in late summer and early autumn. There was hope that most of the potatoes in Ireland could be salvaged. As late as October there was still some optimism. On 1 October, Heytesbury, the Lord Lieutenant, wrote to Graham of reports reaching him that the potato crop in Kilkenny was excellent. Within ten days, however, Heytesbury reported serious cases of crop failure elsewhere. By the end of October, it was only too clear that the failure was extensive.

The ministry was faced with two problems: to find adequate supplies of food, and to create the machinery for its distribution. Both Peel and Graham realised early that only the government could undertake the massive task of feeding a whole population. They also realised that the government must act quickly and that every barrier to the efficient transport of food had to be removed. The most obvious barrier was the restrictive Corn Law. Peel and Graham believed it would be impossible merely to suspend the Corn Law temporarily. Its suspension on the grounds of alleviating scarcity would imply that the government favoured scarcity as a general policy should it be re-imposed. This reason alone argued strongly for Corn Law abolition. Nor would it be possible to open the ports in Ireland to unrestricted grain importation, and yet retain their closure in England. Furthermore, if grain were to be supplied to Ireland by public funds, the public would reasonably expect that the purchase should be made in the cheapest markets, and this could be done only if import barriers were removed.

It remained for Peel and Graham to convert their cabinet colleagues. The cabinet first met to consider the state of Ireland on 31 October 1845. Peel and Graham presented all the information that had reached them. Meeting again the following day, the cabinet heard Peel's recommendations. The first was the establishment of a commission in Ireland that would coordinate famine relief. The cabinet responded favourably, and on 3 November Graham informed Heytesbury of the decision. The Famine Commission (or Scarcity Commission as it was also called) would have wide investigative and remedial authority. Commissioners would include the Head of the Irish Constabulary and the Inspector of the Coast Guard who would use their forces in gathering information. The Head of the Board of Public Works, another Commissioner, would encourage employment of the peasantry on roads, bridges, railways, and drainage projects. To establish food depots and administer the purchase and transport of food was the job of the Commissary in Chief. The distribution of food to the poor from union workhouses would be the responsibility of a new Poor Law Commissioner, the fifth member of the Commission. In his letter to Heytesbury, Graham left open the possibility of appointing some ranking public servant to a sixth position. Peel, always sensitive to matters of this sort, suggested an Irish Catholic for the post because 'we have not one on the Commission'.[3] He named Robert J. Kane, a professor at Queen's College, Cork, who had been engaged on an investigation of the potato blight for the Irish Agricultural Society. Although there were inevitable delays and administrative snags in the early days of the Commission, it had solid achievements to its credit within a few months. These included the establishment of depots for Indian corn, the collection of £100,000 from private and government subscriptions, and the employment of 12,000 labourers a day.

In the meantime, cabinet deliberations had continued on Peel's second recommendation for meeting scarcity in Ireland—the abolition of the Corn Law. The cabinet met frequently throughout November and early December 1845. Parliament was not in session, and it was decided to keep secret the topic under discussion. But, as Wharncliffe ob-

served to Peel, the public was becoming suspicious of so
many cabinet meetings. It was obvious that there was serious
disagreement within the cabinet. Stanley was the firmest
opponent of Corn Law abolition. In early November he
wrote to Peel regretting 'how widely' he differed from him
and Graham on the necessity of Corn Law repeal.[4] Stanley
argued that abolition of the Corn Law was too drastic. He
suggested that the duty on Indian corn only be removed in
order to encourage its importation from North America.
Stanley feared especially the political consequences of Corn
Law abolition: 'our support of the Corn Law', he wrote,
'has been the main inducement to others to give us the support which placed us, and has kept us, in office. . . .'[5] Lord
Lincoln, who represented an agricultural constituency (Nottinghamshire), feared that small farmers would be 'swept
away' by Corn Law repeal.[6] He thought the best course would
be a temporary admittance of some grain in the forthcoming
months, leaving the Corn Law essentially intact. Goulburn
added his doubts to those of his colleagues. He was not
convinced of the failure of the Irish potato crop, believing
it only to be a 'temporary emergency'.[7] Goulburn, like
Stanley, feared the effect of Corn Law abolition upon the
Conservative party. The rank and file would regard its
leadership as traitors and the party would be broken. This
could have disastrous effects on the country: for the Conservative party, Goulburn believed, was 'the only barrier
which remains against the revolutionary effects of the Reform
Bill'.

Peel's attempt to convert his cabinet colleagues reached a
climax during the first week of December. In meetings on
2, 4 and 5 December, Peel brought forward a memorandum
which made specific new proposals altering the Corn Law.
Under the Corn Law of 1842, there had been a duty of 20s
per quarter when domestic prices reached 51s per quarter:
the duty decreased by one shilling for every shilling rise in
the domestic price until only a nominal one shilling duty

remained after domestic wheat reached 73s per quarter. Peel proposed the retention of the sliding scale, but a reduction of the duty from 20s to 8s per quarter. Furthermore, he proposed that in each year following 1846 the duty should be lowered by one shilling, so that within eight years there would be no duty whatsoever: corn would thus, at last, be admitted duty-free. This was a moderate and gradual approach to free trade and it continued the trend of state policy toward grain imports followed by successive governments since 1828. But it was not well received in the cabinet. Two cabinet ministers—Stanley and Buccleuch—threatened to resign over the issue: of the remainder, most supported Peel only reluctantly. In the light of the opinion of these, his closest supporters, Peel knew it was very unlikely that he could carry through Parliament any relaxation of the Corn Laws, much less their abolition. On 5 December, Peel tendered the seals of office to the Queen. It seemed that the ministry was at an end.

During the ministerial deliberations, the Whigs had been manoeuvring to take what political advantage they could of the apparent division within the cabinet. They were fearful that the ministry might ultimately decide to steal a march on the Whig position on the Corn Laws. As Palmerston warned Lord John Russell: 'If he [Peel] takes your fixed Duty Measure, he will not have left us a shirt to our backs'.[8] To preclude any such move on the part of the ministry, Lord John published his *Letter to the Electors of the City of London* on 22 November 1845. In it he announced his conversion to Corn Law repeal, with the strong implication that this was also the line to be adopted by the Whigs in the next session of Parliament (although Russell had not, in fact, consulted his colleagues on this matter). By placing the Whig position first before the public, Lord John could claim —should the Conservative ministry come to similar free-trade conclusions—to have prodded the ministry into action. Lord John thus gained what he hoped would be a useful political initiative, while simultaneously poising the Whigs for action in the event of the ministry's division proving fatal to its continuance. When the ministry resigned within two weeks of the publication of the *Letter*, it seemed that Russell's gamble would pay off.

Unfortunately for Russell, he had not calculated very precisely the consequences of his action. By committing himself to free trade before the meeting of parliament, he would only alert the protectionists. If protectionist sentiment were strong enough to bring down Peel's ministry, what guarantee was there that it would not bring down a Whig ministry? Therefore, Russell negotiated through third parties for Peel's support for a Whig free-trade proposal. Although Peel was unwilling (naturally enough) to pledge himself to a specific measure, he indicated his willingness to support a general settlement of the Corn Law question that looked toward abolition.

Russell was engaged not only in finding support for Corn Law abolition outside Whig ranks, but in negotiating as well among his Whig colleagues for a viable cabinet. He soon discovered that two whom he considered indispensable could not be joined in a single cabinet. The cantankerous and radical-minded Earl Grey objected to the inclusion of Lord Palmerston at the Foreign Office.[9] Grey was explicit in his objection in a letter to Russell: during Palmerston's previous tenure at the Foreign Office, events occurred which were 'by no means forgotten' among diplomats and statesmen of the world and 'more especially of France'.[10] Grey suggested that Palmerston be given the Colonial Office instead: otherwise, Grey told Russell, he would be unable to join the cabinet. Grey had been so prominent in free-trade advocacy that Russell could not omit him from a free-trade ministry. To exclude Palmerston from the cabinet would be equally unthinkable. Palmerston was determined to accept no other than the Foreign Office—a resolve strengthened by the news of Grey's objections. The problem of cabinet-making seemed

insoluble. As Russell explained to the Queen in his letter of
20 December 1845 relinquishing his attempt to form a ministry, a division among his colleagues in a government destined
to be a minority one at the outset did not augur well for its
continuance. Peel was again summoned by the Queen.

The failure of Lord John's attempt to form a government
transformed the prospects of the Peel ministry. It was obvious that there was no alternative to Peel. Except for Stanley, who resigned, the cabinet now supported Peel. It seems
the cabinet came round to Wellington's opinion that 'good
government for the country is more important than Corn
Laws. . . .'[11] In addition to Stanley's departure, one other
cabinet position fell open with the almost unnoticed death
during Russell's negotiations of the President of the Council,
Lord Wharncliffe. Peel used the opportunities thus offered
to strengthen the cabinet. Gladstone, having served enough
time in the wilderness to satisfy his conscience over Maynooth, replaced Stanley at the Colonial Office. Lord Eliot,
former Chief Secretary of Ireland, and now Earl of St Germans, took the Post Office; Ellenborough was given the
Admiralty; and Dalhousie, President of the Board of Trade
since Gladstone's departure but without cabinet rank, was
advanced to the cabinet. The Whigs, so hopeful only days
before, ruefully recognised Peel's enhanced ministerial prospects. Palmerston observed to Lord John that Peel had 'on
the whole mended his position by resigning, for he has gained
some good Recruits for his Cabinet, and having taken the
benefit of the act, he is free from his former entanglements
and sets up business as a new man'.[12]

A strengthened ministry was necessary to oppose the
protectionists. Even before Parliament met on 22 January
1846, protectionist quarters were in arms. Lord Redesdale
bitterly complained to Ellenborough of the 'insane conduct'
of Peel and threatened to go into opposition if Peel persisted
in it.[13] The Duke of Rutland wrote to Wellington that the
ministerial change of policy on the Corn Laws was 'danger-

ous' because it was a 'species of genuflexion' toward the Anti-Corn Law League.[14] Lord George Bentinck, a younger son of the Duke of Portland, condemned Peel and his colleagues as 'no better than common cheats' and recommended that their ears be cropped and they be placed in the pillory as a suitable punishment.[15]

No less outraged than these scions of the aristocracy were the farmers. Farmers believed that the Conservative victory in 1841 had carried the pledge of protection. The countryside had voted overwhelmingly in that election against the liberalisation of the Corn Law proposed by the Whig ministry. For Peel to go beyond even the Whig proposal of 1841 and adopt the League's demands for free trade was intolerable. In December 1845, protectionist farmers, led by the so-called Anti-League, campaigned against the ministry's free-trade proposal. It was an unprecedented outpouring of protectionist sentiment, far overshadowing the protectionist campaign of 1842. In meetings and through petitions, farmers brought pressure to bear on their MPs to stand firm on the Corn Laws. Some flavour of the campaign may be suggested by example. The *Essex Standard* and the *Lincolnshire Chronicle* were two of the staunchest protectionist journals in the kingdom, and represented two of the most famous farming counties. Their pages, which reported numerous protectionist meetings, furnished unhappy reading for Peel and his supporters. At a meeting of the Horncastle Agricultural Protection Society, for example, a John Ellwood of Mareham condemned Peel's actions as those of a 'traitor': Peel had, he said, 'come into office on the shoulders of the agriculturists', yet since the election, Peel 'had continually reduced and frittered down the protection the farmers had hitherto enjoyed. . . .' Ellwood urged protectionists to 'watch the votes and conduct of their representatives' to keep them 'firm in the performance of their duty to their agricultural constituents. . . .'[16] At the Rutland Agricultural Protection Society, there was talk of uniting protectionists of the land with other interests, such as the colonial, which might also be threatened by free trade.[17] The Spalding Agricultural Protection meeting adopted 'No Surrender' as their motto, and declared that 'Sir R. Peel had deserted them at an awful moment'.[18] Similar speeches were made at agricultural meetings in Essex. More significant action was taken at the Essex Agricultural Protection Society when £2,000 was voted to support a campaign for the retention of the Corn Laws.[19] As a result of the Conservative leadership's change of heart on the Corn Laws, the *Essex Standard* recommended that its readers 'discard the old distinctions of party: these have become obsolete. . . . We are now divided into protectionists and Leaguers'.[20] The rising chorus of criticism against Peel was heard far beyond the more fertile regions of agriculture. Even in Cornwall, the editor of the Conservative *Cornwall Royal Gazette* tried to trace the motives which led Peel to a policy 'by which he had lost character as well as power'.[21]

As the date for the parliamentary session approached, protectionist pressure increased. Over thirty local protectionist associations met in January and February 1846. Some of these meetings decided to seek protectionist pledges from their MPs. By late January, several MPs who felt they could not uphold protection were forced to resign. Among these was Lord Ashley at Dorset. Protectionist wrath among the electorate even struck down members of the government. Sir Thomas Fremantle, who had replaced Eliot as Chief Secretary for Ireland in January 1845, was convinced by his experience in Ireland that the Corn Law would contribute to the scarcity of food in Ireland. Fremantle represented Buckingham, which lay within the zone of influence of the protectionist Duke of Buckingham. The Duke, who had resigned from the cabinet over the tariff bill of 1842, no doubt exerted some pressure on Fremantle. But, as Fremantle informed Graham, the real pressure came from his angered constituents. Graham relayed the information to

Heytesbury: 'the electors of Buckingham', he wrote, 'have driven Fremantle into a corner. . . .'[22] Lord Lincoln, who succeeded Fremantle in Ireland after the latter's resignation in January 1846, had no better luck with his constituents. Standing for Nottinghamshire after his appointment, Lincoln was severely beaten in a contest in which his father, the protectionist Duke of Newcastle, had used his influence against him. Lincoln was unable to find a seat until May, almost at the end of Peel's term of office. One of the most disheartening by-election results was at Westminster where the Peelite Captain H. J. Rous lost to a free-trade Whig, Sir George de Lacy Evans. In explaining his defeat to Peel, Rous declared that 'the Whig Rads & Leaguers combined. The Tories were neuter or canvassed agt. me. . . . D'Israeli in full dress uniform, Lord J Russell in simple Toga, & a Leaguer in rags met & polled together for Evans at the same booth'.[23] In addition to by-election defeats, the ministry was faced with protest resignations from some of the minor Household posts, and from the Treasury and Admiralty. It was a worrying trend, as Peel admitted in a letter to his brother in late January.[24]

Peel and his colleagues had underestimated the strength of local protectionist sentiment. By ignoring the representatives of rural constituents, Peel made a serious tactical mistake. It is not surprising that he overlooked them, for he had a low opinion of their abilities. But by leaving the country members out of account during the policy discussions prior to the opening of Parliament, he did not even afford them, as one MP complained, 'the common courtesy' of consultation.[25] This placed the country members in an awkward position when they faced their constituents during the early hectic days of the Corn Law debates. Since Peel had not consulted them and confided in them the reasons for Corn Law repeal, they had little choice but to conform to their constituents' demands. Peel's treatment of his backbenchers during the early weeks of the Corn Law crisis broke the

majority's loyalty. It was the culmination of years of bad
feeling which had begun in the early days of the ministry.
Had Peel been less aloof and more accommodating, the
ensuing bitterness and party divisions might well have been
avoided.

The personal attacks by the protectionists on the Prime
Minister heard in the countryside were echoed in the extended and often fierce parliamentary debates of the following months. The tone was set on the first day of the new
session during the debate on the Queen's Speech. The protectionist peer and head of the Anti-League, the Duke of
Richmond, claimed to see no difference between the ministry
and the Anti-Corn Law League, and mused aloud as to why
Cobden should not be made a peer. In a more truculent
mood, he threatened to 'use every Parliamentary means of
opposition' to prevent the abolition of protection.[26]

Peel was undeterred by protectionist anger. Outlining
his new tariff policy in the first week of the session, he proceeded 'on the assumption that protective duties, abstracted-
ly and on principle', were objectionable.[27] Thus he widened
the potential benefit of free trade from Ireland alone to the
whole of the kingdom. He pointed out the falling crime rates
and the increasing social stability in the country since the
revised Corn Law of 1842. 'Is it possible', he asked the
House, 'to resist the inference that employment, low prices,
comparative abundance, contribute to the diminution of
crime?'[28] Yet this had been achieved without the loss of
profit to domestic producers. He cited statistics showing
that in some cases imports had not been as great as feared
under the 1842 Corn Law. He cited others showing that
even where imports had increased substantially, there had
been no loss to the agriculturists.

The heart of the new proposal was the abolition of all
duties on imported corn after February 1849. Until then,
there would be a duty of 10s per quarter when domestic
corn was less than 48s a quarter, diminishing to 4s when the

price rose to 53s and above. Although it was slightly less generous toward the agriculturists than the original proposal to the cabinet in December, the scheme had retained its gradualist character. There was a great deal more to the proposal than mere Corn Law abolition. It immediately repealed duties on salt and fresh pork, live cattle, and all vegetables, and reduced butter and cheese duties. The differential between colonial 'free' sugar and slave-grown sugar was reduced. Peel's tariff reductions affected more than imported foodstuffs. As in 1842, he reduced or abolished duties on a large number of manufactured goods ranging from textiles to timber and shoes to soap. For example, the 10 percent duty on rough cotton goods was abolished, and the duty on foreign shoes was halved from 14s to 7s the dozen pairs.

Peel also proposed several measures of compensation to the landed classes, including the reduction of seed duties and the free import of maize and buckwheat. This would reduce the cost of fattening cattle and give the stock farmer, as Peel put it, 'increased facilities for meeting foreign competition'.[29] Arable farmers would be provided for by state loans at low interest rates for the improvement of agricultural practices. Further compensatory measures included the assumption by the public treasury of various expenses previously borne by the localities: the prosecution and maintenance of prisoners, and the expenses of Poor Law medical officers, schoolteachers, and auditors. The highway rate would be lessened by consolidating local highway administration from the 16,000 local authorities to only 600. The law of settlement, which had allowed urban authorities to return the unemployed poor to their original rural residences during depression times, would be abolished, thus lessening the poor rate in the countryside. The lightening of these local burdens, borne to a great extent by the farmers, would, Peel hoped, make them more amenable to Corn Law repeal.

The tariff scheme of 1846 was the culmination of the ministry's attempt to bring orderly growth and social stability to Britain. It was a neatly complementary package which simultaneously reduced the cost of living, especially of the poor, compensated the farmers, and gave manufacturers cheaper raw material. By stilling the voice of the Anti-Corn Law League, Peel also hoped to reduce further the level of public tension and class division. In Peel's eyes, the most important of these aims was a contribution toward the living standards of the mass of the population. Nothing was more essential to a well-ordered state. To a Conservative colleague, he wrote: 'I have seen the effect of a moderate price of provisions—improved manufactures—extended employment—buoyant Revenue—decrease of Crime—Social Contentment—and I do honestly and sincerely dread the consequences of advanced prices, and a resolute maintenance of the present Corn Laws.'[30]

Peel's emphasis on the social benefits of free trade gave his protectionist opponents reason to think that the Irish crisis was merely a pretext for Corn Law repeal. They did not believe that the Irish potato blight was as serious as Peel had depicted. Even a long speech by Peel quoting extensively from Irish documents failed to convince. Nor did they believe that the compensations offered would enable farmers to meet successfully the lower price of foreign agricultural produce on the domestic market. George Bankes, the protectionist member for Dorset, denounced the compensations as 'trifling'.[31] Most galling to the protectionists was the change in Peel's mind about the Corn Law, and his 'treason' to the party. During the debate on the Queen's Speech, Peel candidly admitted to the House that he had changed his mind, and that his proposals were 'the worst measures for party interests that could have been brought forward'.[32] To the protectionists, the abandonment of protection was tantamount to abandonment of the Conservative party. They hinted broadly that Peel ought to resign his leadership. No leader of a party, A. J. B. Hope (Maidstone) told the House of Commons, was in that position 'by divine hereditary

right'.[33] At the very least, Peel should go to the country on
the tariff scheme. But Peel was determined that the issue
should be settled in Parliament and not at the polls. The idea
of a referendum was foreign to his political philosophy.

The protectionists did not merely complain about Peel
to Parliament. On 9 February 1846, they implemented the
Duke of Richmond's implied threat of delay. P. W. Skinner
Miles (Bristol) moved an amendment asking for a six-month
postponement. The debate lasted twelve nights. Of more than
a hundred speakers, half were protectionists. As customarily
silent Conservative backbenchers fired salvo after salvo at
their leader, intemperate language rose. It culminated on 27
February with the first speech of Lord George Bentinck
(King's Lynn), soon to be the acknowledged leader of the
protectionists. Dismissing the 'pretended' potato famine,
Lord George staggered the House with a mass of statistics
to prove the protectionist case. In concluding his speech,
he observed that the landed interest, in contrast to the party
leadership, would never be guilty of 'double-dealing with the
farmers of England—of swindling our opponents, deceiving
our friends, or betraying our constituents'.[34] The vote at
the end of Bentinck's speech on Miles' amendment was
337 against and 240 for. It was a comfortable enough
majority of 97. But an examination of the votes held an
ominous portent for the ministry. Of 337 voting for the
ministry, only 112 were Conservatives. Two-thirds of the
Conservative party had deserted Peel. The protectionists
continued their delaying tactics but were unsuccessful in
preventing the bill's second reading in late March. During
the third reading in May, the personal attacks on Peel
grew in intensity, reaching a climax with Disraeli's speech
during the final night of the debate. To the support of
protectionist cheers, Disraeli declared that Peel's political
life was nothing more than 'one great appropriation clause'
and that he had always 'traded on the ideas and intelligence
of others. . . .' The rest of the party leadership was little

better: Disraeli described them as 'political pedlars that bought their party in the cheapest market, and sold us in the dearest'.[35] However, Disraeli's voicing of authentic backbencher anguish could not overcome the Whig–Peelite combination. The bill was given its third reading, and sent to the House of Lords.

While Corn Law repeal was making its way through Parliament, the ministry was also pushing forward other Irish measures. In March, it introduced the Fever Bill, which would create a Board of Health in Dublin to supervise the construction of fever hospitals and to provide medical assistance to those suffering from fever arising from the scarcity. More controversial was the Protection of Life Bill. It also proved to be the most crucial measure of the session, for its defeat in the House of Commons brought an end to Peel's ministry.

The Protection of Life Bill was introduced in the House of Lords by St Germans in February. It aimed at pacifying Ireland, and was a retreat to the coercionist policy of 1843. Disorders in Ireland had spread during the winter to such an extent that the ministry felt compelled to act. The proposal would empower the Lord Lieutenant to proclaim disturbed districts and increase their police forces as necessary. Curfews at night would be enforced, and infractions punished by sentences of up to seven years' transportation. Compensation for victims of outrages would be met by a fine upon the residents of the district involved. It was a harsh measure, though no more so than the Whig Irish Coercion Act of 1833. Apart from the criticism of Earl Grey, there was little opposition to the proposal in the House of Lords.

When the bill reached the House of Commons in late March, it faced an initially small opposition. Only the Irish liberals seemed united against it. O'Connell and William Smith O'Brien were among the most vociferous in debate, and engaged in obstructive tactics by calling for frequent adjournments. Apart from this expected Irish opposition,

other groups in the House seemed to support the first
reading. But their reasons for doing so held little promise for
the bill. The protectionists supported it because the ensuing
debate would inevitably delay Corn Law repeal. Thus, they
happily acquiesced in the obstructionist tactics of the Irish
members. Lord John Russell did not favour the bill and had
been displeased with the Whig peers' support of it. Yet Russell did not want to jeopardise Peel's ministry until the Corn
Law had been repealed. This led him to temporise during the
early stages of the Protection of Life Bill, speaking in favour
of its first reading, while reserving his options in the later
stages. Should there be a conjunction of protectionist and
Whig sentiments against the bill (as there was now in its
favour), the ministry would be defeated.

As coercion and corn absorbed parliamentary energies
throughout April and May, political uncertainties were
increased by rumours of various coalitions. A well-founded
one was a projected alliance between Irish Whig peers and
Conservative protectionist peers. This unlikely combination
was motivated by the growing distaste for the disorders in
Ireland among the Irish peers. Desiring a coercion bill, they
were willing to compromise on Corn Law repeal, if the protectionists would support coercion. This would, however,
nullify Whig policy as set out by Lord John Russell in his
letter of November 1845, which had publicly committed the
Whigs to free trade. To counter the peers' revolt, Lord John
convened them at Lansdowne House on 23 May. In an unaccustomed display of decisiveness, he threatened resignation
as party leader if they voted against Peel's Corn Law measure.
The revolt collapsed, and the coalition with the protectionists
was quashed.

Lord John's action had three important consequences. It
gave the Whigs, for the first time in years, a party unity. It
removed the last obstruction to Corn Law abolition. And it
removed any reason among the protectionists for delay on
the Protection of Life Bill. When, therefore, debate began in

the House of Commons on the second reading of the Protection of Life Bill in early June, Bentinck announced that
the protectionists had decided to reverse themselves and
to oppose it. Bentinck was nothing if not blunt. He told the
House 'that the sooner we kick out the Bill and Her Majesty's
Ministers together the better'.[36] On 25 June, after several
adjourned debates, the House voted against the second reading of the bill. An uneasy combination of Whigs, Irish liberals, Leaguers, and protectionists had turned out the Peel
ministry by a vote of 292–219. Peel had the satisfaction of
seeing half the protectionists vote for the coercion bill. Their
anti-Irish feeling had overcome a factious desire to oppose
on this occasion. There were enough protectionists among
the remainder, however, who followed Bentinck in the division lobby to make the difference against the ministry.

The defeat left the ministry with two alternatives. It
could appeal to the country in a general election, or resign.
It chose the latter. As Graham explained to Heytesbury, an
election would not be advisable in view of the volatile condition of Ireland. In any case, the Corn Bill was safe. 'In
short, our Mission for good is nearly closed.'[37] Four days
after the adverse vote on the Protection of Life Bill, Peel
gave his resignation speech to the House of Commons. In it,
he paid unusual tribute to the man who, he said, would be
longer remembered than he as responsible for the repeal of
the Corn Law—Richard Cobden. This was a curious
reference, for it unnecessarily detracted from Peel's own
achievement, and it seemed a gratuitous insult to protectionists and Whigs alike, although for different reasons.
It was also curious in that Peel can scarcely be counted as
a supporter of the Anti-Corn Law League. Peel himself
declared that he meant his words to apply to Cobden's
activity inside Parliament.[38] It may be that Peel was
responding to Cobden's own tribute to Peel, delivered prior
to the crucial vote on the Protection of Life Bill a few nights
earlier. In his speech, Cobden had dissociated himself from

his temporary allies, the protectionists. Indeed, his speech was almost an apology for voting against Peel. Cobden declared that Peel carried with him 'the esteem and gratitude of a larger number of the population of this Empire than ever followed any Minister that was ever hurled from power'. Cobden offered to Peel his own 'heartfelt thanks for the unwearied perseverance, the unswerving firmness, and the great ability' with which he repealed the Corn Law.[39]

It was a fitting parliamentary tribute and it is not surprising that Peel should have responded in kind. Cobden's was one of the few marks of appreciation that Peel had heard in Parliament for many months. Subjected to almost daily taunts from the protectionists, he had lived under a steady campaign of personal vilification such as has rarely been seen in the modern House of Commons. The protectionists, from their point of view, had been right to try to break Peel. Without Peel, it is unlikely that Corn Law repeal would have been successful in 1846. Of course, it had not been his achievement alone. He had been closely seconded by Graham, and in the later stages of the debates Lord John had lent timely assistance. But it had been Peel who, since late 1845 when the first rumours of scarcity reached England, had provided the determination to relieve Ireland. It was this determination that won the cabinet to a policy of Corn Law repeal.

The repeal of the Corn Law was once considered to be the triumph of the middle class over the aristocracy, thus completing a legislative trend begun in 1832 with electoral reform. The Anti-Corn Law League, one of the first of the modern political pressure groups, has been held to be the main instrument of this success. Modern research has proved this a simplistic view. As we have seen, the League had little influence in the decisions of the Peel ministry. Peel saw Corn Law repeal as an Irish measure, set within a broader framework of the need to promote public order and social stability. Nor can repeal be seen merely as a struggle between the commercial middle classes and the landed interest. If this were so, Corn Law repeal would never have passed the House of Commons, 80 percent of which was comprised of men related to the aristocracy and gentry. And it must be remembered that the House of Lords, a wholly aristocratic body, offered less resistance to Corn Law repeal than the House of Commons. Class interests alone cannot account for Corn Law repeal. Some of the landed interest had been genuinely converted to the principles of free trade. Others trusted Peel. The lure of office persuaded others to relinquish protectionist tendencies. For a variety of reasons, the time for free trade had come.

Epilogue

Peel never again held public office. Nor did he take an active part in Conservative party politics after 1846. In spite of numerous appeals from the non-protectionist members of the Conservative party, Peel refused to assume any position of leadership. The bruising attacks made upon him by members of his own party during the Corn Law debates had deeply affected him. As he informed his friends, he did not regret his expulsion from office. Indeed, he rejoiced in it as a relief from 'an intolerable burden'.[1] He was relieved to be freed from a party, many members of which, he said (referring to the protectionists), spent their time 'eating and drinking and hunting, shooting, gambling, horseracing, and so forth' instead of attending to the affairs of government. This harsh and not wholly justified opinion was strongly enough held by Peel and his following to preclude any reconciliation of the two wings of the party during Peel's lifetime.

Feeling as he did, Peel was often more friendly in Parliament toward the Whigs than toward the majority of the party which he had led so long. Peel never avoided an opportunity of supporting the Whig ministry in its defence of free trade after 1846. The revival of protection in the years following Corn Law repeal was a distinct possibility. As agricultural prices slumped in the late 1840s, farmers and country MPs once again agitated for higher protectionist duties. There were even rumours that some members of the Whig cabinet were thinking of restoring some protection on agricultural imports in the shape of a fixed duty.[2] In February 1850 the Whigs only narrowly overcame a protectionist motion sponsored by Disraeli. The vote was 273–252: Peel and 27 of his supporters had provided the margin of victory. In the previous year, Peel had also supported the Whigs on the repeal of the Navigation Laws. Thus Peel, even though out of office, contributed to the maintenance of a free-trade policy and consolidated one of the most important achievements of his ministry.

Peel also made a significant contribution to Whig fiscal policy, a traditional Whig weakness. The Whig Chancellor of the Exchequer, Sir Charles Wood, established a close working relationship with Peel. The two met on occasion to discuss fiscal difficulties, and Wood often sent Peel official financial papers. A friendly correspondence developed between the two on a large number of topics. Once, during the commercial crisis of 1847, Peel actually drafted a letter for Wood suggesting a ministerial policy toward the Bank of England. Lord John Russell, in turn, directed that the official papers on the crisis be shown to Peel.[3] It was a remarkable recognition of Peel's expertise in financial matters, and a striking demonstration of the esteem in which he was held even by his political opponents.

Another member of Russell's cabinet, the Earl of Clarendon, Lord Lieutenant of Ireland from 1847, also consulted Peel on matters of state. Between Clarendon and Peel existed a sympathy for Irish problems that prompted a candid exchange of opinions. Peel believed that the famine, by cruelly exposing Ireland's deep-rooted social and economic defects, provided a unique opportunity for settling the Irish question. An added opportunity was provided by the death of O'Connell at Genoa in 1847, while he was on a pilgrimmage to Rome. Peel believed that England should fill the vacuum in the Irish leadership by taking the initiative with a comprehensive legislative programme. In a memorandum given to Clarendon in April 1849, Peel outlined his plan.[4] He proposed a government commission with extensive powers of social administration, including the superintendence of emigration and public works. More importantly, the commission would be responsible for the management and improvement of Irish encumbered estates. The commission, additionally, would facilitate the sale of encumbered estates to purchasers who would, Peel hoped, be more willing to act as improvers on the land. But the plan seemed too great an interference with the rights of property. The Whigs limited themselves to the immediate needs of famine relief, and another opportunity was lost in Ireland.

It is impossible to know what Peel's position might have become had he lived longer. Very likely, he would have continued in the role of a senior statesman, acting in what he considered to be the national interest, regardless of party. His unexpected death on 2 July 1850, three days after a riding accident near Constitution Hill, came at the height of his national reputation. During his last years, he had continued to play a constructive parliamentary role. He became almost an Olympian figure, giving advice to all who sought it. Perhaps only in his indifference to party did he fail to play a constructive role. From 1846 to 1850 he contributed significantly to a state of suspended animation in the party system, as one historian has noted.[5] Even for some years after 1850, the party system was in abeyance. Not until the emergence of a reconstructed Conservative party, shorn of its protectionism, was the party system again strengthened. The later political careers of Peel's own ministers attest to the shattering impact of the crisis of 1846 on party. Stanley ultimately led a protectionist ministry; Aberdeen formed a coalition government, joined by Graham; and Gladstone drifted to the left to dominate the Liberal party in the last half of the century. If it left no legacy to party government, Peel's administration nevertheless bequeathed much to the nation. Its cautious foreign policy preserved peace abroad. Its solid achievements in commercial reform helped shape the forthcoming decades of mid-Victorian prosperity and political stability. In the long run, perhaps the most important

bequest to future administrations was the ministry's emphasis on fiscal responsibility and executive efficiency. It was a
model that every future administration might hope to follow.

Notes

INTRODUCTION (pages 7-13)

1 Norman Gash's two-volume life of Peel
2 Matthews, R. C. O. *A Study in Trade-Cycle History: Economic Fluctuations in Great Britain, 1833-1842* (Cambridge, 1954), *passim*, esp 214-17
3 For the above figures, see Hobsbawm, E. J. *Labouring Men* (London, 1964), 74-5
4 Ibid
5 Patterson, A. Temple. *Radical Leicester: A History of Leicester 1780-1850* (Leicester, 1954), 327
6 Pollard, Sidney. *A History of Labour in Sheffield* (Liverpool, 1959), 40
7 Flinn, M. W. (ed). *Edwin Chadwick's Report on the Sanitary Condition of the Labouring Population of Great Britain* (Edinburgh, 1965), 13
8 Hamburger, Joseph. *James Mill and the Art of Revolution* (New Haven and London, 1963), esp chap 3. Hamburger makes a general case for the lack of revolutionary conditions in the early 1830s
9 For this paragraph see: Beer, Samuel H. 'The Representation of Interests in British Government: Historical Background', *American Political Science Review*, Vol LI, No 3 (Sept 1957), 613-50; Fraser, Peter. 'Public Petitioning and Parliament before 1832', *History*, Vol XLVI, No 158 (Oct 1961), 195-211; Lucas, B. Keith. 'County Meetings', *Law Quarterly Review*, Vol LXX (Jan 1954), 109-14

Chapter 1 THE ELECTION AND THE NEW MINISTRY (pages 17-44)

1 *Morning Chronicle*, 1 July 1841
2 For the Budget and the ensuing debate, see *Hansard*, LVII, 1295-1372, 30 April 1841
3 Ibid, 1335, 30 April 1841
4 Ibid, LVIII, 639, 18 May 1841
5 Gash, Norman. *Politics in the Age of Peel* (London, 1953), xiii
6 Hanham, H. J. 'Ashburton as a Parliamentary Borough', *The Devonshire Association for the Advancement of Science, Literature and Art, Report and Transactions*, Vol XCVIII (1966), 206-56

7   *Staffordshire Advertiser*, 3 July 1841. This was John Quincey Harris
    who won 166 votes of the 269 feltmakers voting, including 62 plump-
    ers (calculated from *An Alphabetical Copy of the Poll . . . of . . .
    the Borough of Newcastle-under-Lyme* (Newcastle-under-Lyme,
    1841). Harris was, however, removed by petition in 1842 on charges
    of bribery and a Conservative ultimately took his place

8   See, for example, Davis, Richard W. *Political Change and Con-
    tinuity, 1760-1885: A Buckinghamshire Study* (Newton Abbot, 1972)

9   *The Times*, 25 May 1841

10 Reeve, Henry (ed). *The Greville Memoirs: A Journal of the Reign of
    Queen Victoria* (New York, 1885), I, 359

11 Blake, Robert. *The Conservative Party from Peel To Churchill*
    (New York, 1970), 44-9

12 Ibid, 46

13 *Berks Chronicle*, 3 July 1841. Professor Gash notes the importance
    of the Corn Law issue to Reading in 1841: 'Though it was an urban
    commercial community with a strong dissenting leaven, it was also
    a market town, the centre of a predominantly farming country, and
    bound by close links to the soil.' (Gash, *Politics in the Age of Peel*,
    294). There was apparently some bribery as well at Reading, and a
    general disorganisation among the local Whigs which contributed to
    their defeat (Ibid, 295-300)

14 *Cambridge Chronicle*, 3 July 1841. The spokesman was R. M. Faw-
    cett, in support of the Conservative Manners Sutton

15 See Vincent, J. R. *Pollbooks: How Victorians Voted* (Cambridge,
    1967), chap I, where a case is made for occupational homogeneity
    in voting patterns; see also Nossiter, T. J. 'Shopkeeper Radicalism in
    the 19th Century', in Nossiter, T. J., Hanson, A. H., and Rokkan,
    Stein (eds). *Imagination and Precision in the Social Sciences* (Lon-
    don, 1972), 407-38

16 Calculated from *A Correct List of the Voters . . . for the Borough
    of Reading* (Reading, 1841)

17 The 1835 information is from Vincent, *Pollbooks*, 86; the 1841
    information is calculated from *The Poll . . . Cambridge* (29 June
    1841). The influence of Cambridge University upon the borough
    electorate cannot be overlooked (see Gash, *Politics in the Age of
    Peel*, 174)

18 Neale, R. S. *Class and Ideology in the Nineteenth Century*, (London
    and Boston, 1972), chap 3

19 Blake, *Conservative Party*, 46

20 *Liverpool Courier*, 30 June 1841

21 Calculated from the *Poll Book . . . for the Borough of Liverpool
    1841* (Liverpool, 1841)

22 *Bristol Gazette*, 2 June 1841

23 Calculated from the *Bristol Poll Book* (Bristol, 1841)

24 *Essex Standard*, 9 July 1841

25 Russell Papers, PRO 30/22/4B, f 21, Morpeth to Russell, 9 July 1841
26 Thompson, F. M. L. 'Whigs and Liberals in the West Riding', *English Historical Review*, Vol LXXIV (1959), 214-39
27 *Leeds Mercury*, 5 June 1841
28 Ibid, 23 June 1841
29 Ibid, 29 May 1841
30 Thompson, 'Whigs and Liberals in the West Riding', 223
31 Russell Papers, PRO 30/22/4B, f 21, Morpeth to Russell, 9 July 1841
32 Church, Roy A. *Economic and Social Change in a Midland Town: Victorian Nottingham, 1815-1900* (London, Frank Cass reprint, 1966), chaps 5 and 6; Thomis, Malcolm I. *Politics and Society in Nottingham, 1785-1835* (New York, 1969), chap 8; Wood A. C. 'Nottingham, 1835-1865', *Transactions of the Thoroton Society of Nottinghamshire*, Vol LIX (1955), 1-83; Wyncoll, Peter. *Nottingham Chartism* (Nottingham, 1966)
33 *Nottingham Review*, 2 April 1841
34 *Nottingham Mercury*, 18 June 1841
35 Approximately 20 percent of the Nottingham electorate who voted in the by-election were framework knitters—728 of a total of 3,728: 366 of these voted for Walter and 362 for Larpent (calculated from *An Alphabetical List of the Burgesses, Occupiers, and Freeholders who polled at the election of a Burgess to Represent the Town of Nottingham . . . April 1841* (Nottingham, nd)
36 Hughenden MSS, B/1/B/6, 26 May 1841, C. H. Frewen MP to Disraeli
37 *Ipswich Journal*, 26 June 1841. Kelly, however, lost
38 Boyson, Rhodes. *The Ashworth Cotton Enterprise: the Rise and Fall of a Family Firm, 1818-1880* (Oxford, 1970), 160-1
39 *Staffordshire Advertiser*, 29 May 1841
40 *North Staffordshire Mercury*, 22 May 1841
41 *Leicester Mercury*, 5 June 1841
42 *York Herald*, 26 June 1841
43 *Bristol Gazette*, 27 May 1841
44 Harney and Pitkeithly later withdrew their candidacy to avoid election costs: Schoyen, A. R. *The Chartist Challenge: A Portrait of George Julian Harney* (New York, 1958), 107-8
45 *Northampton Mercury*, 17 July 1841: the *Mercury* was whiggishly inclined. See also the pollbook, *Northampton Borough Election* (nd)
46 For this discussion of Bradford, see Peacock, A. J. 'Bradford Chartism, 1838-1840', *Borthwick Papers*, No 36 (York, 1969), and Wright, D. G. 'A Radical Borough: Parliamentary Politics in Bradford, 1832-1841,' *Northern History,* Vol IV (1969), 132-66. A report in the *York Herald*, 3 July 1841, confirms the importance of the Chartist vote to Hardy
47 *Leeds Mercury*, 29 May 1841

48   *Nottingham Review*, 30 April 1841
49   *Northern Star*, 19 June 1841
50   *Leicester Mercury*, 29 May 1841
51·   See the *Leicester Mercury*, 10 July 1841, for the South Leicester
      nomination day proceedings, and the *Leicester Journal*, 23 July
      1841, for the Conservative victory dinner
52   *Carlisle Patriot*, 26 June 1841 and 3 July 1841
53   *Birmingham Journal*, 10 July 1841
54   See the accounts in the *Norfolk Chronicle*, 3 July 1841, and the
      Norwich Mercury, 3 July 1841
55   Peel Papers, Add Ms 40474, f 254, Peel to Hardinge, 24 Mar 1845
56   Ibid, 40467, ff 226-7, Peel to Stanley, 28 Aug 1842
57   Ibid, 40584, ff 180-1, Peel to Shirley Palmer, 4 Feb 1846
58   Ibid, 40472, f 104, Peel to Ellenborough, 1 Nov 1843
59   Hodder, Edwin. *The Life and Work of the Seventh Earl of Shaftes-
      bury, K. G.* (London, 1886), I, 341
60   Parker, Charles Stuart (ed). *Sir Robert Peel* (London, 1899), II,
      Peel to Graham, 2 Sept 1842, 543
61   Ibid, Peel to Croker, 3 Aug 1842, 530
62   *Greville Memoirs*, II, 333
63   Peel Papers, Add Ms 40446, ff 9-16, Graham to Peel, 1 Aug 1841
64   As he called it in a letter to Peel (Ibid, 40451, ff 328-9, 30 Sept 1845)
65   Ibid, 40449, f 111, Graham to Peel, 20 Oct 1843
66   Mather, F. C. *Public Order in the Age of the Chartists* (Manchester,
      1959), 43
67   *Hansard*, LXV, 909, 1 Aug 1842
68   Peel Papers, Add Ms 40448, f 326, Graham to Peel, 18 June 1843
69   Ibid, 40459, ff 105-6, Peel to Wellington, 17 Dec 1841
70   As Professor Gash has observed in his *Peel*, II, 286
71   Ellenborough Papers, PRO 30/12/21/7, Ellenborough to Hardinge,
      24 Mar 1846.
72   Jones, Wilbur Devereux. *'Prosperity' Robinson: the Life of Viscount
      Goderich, 1782-1859* (New York, 1967)
73   Peel Papers, Add Ms 40464, ff 48-9, Peel to Ripon, 30 Oct 1841. For
      Ripon's letters to Peel see ibid, ff 27 ff, 7 Oct 1841; ff 33 ff, 19 Oct
      1841; and ff 44 ff, 29 Oct 1841
74   Hammond, J. L., and Foot, M. R. D. *Gladstone and Liberalism*
      (New York, Collier Paperback, 1966), 37
75   Peel Papers, Add Ms 40450, f 317, Peel to Graham, 5 Nov 1844
76   See, for example, Sir Charles Webster's judgement in *The Foreign
      Policy of Palmerston, 1830-1841* (London, 1951), II, 790
77   Peel Papers, Add Ms 40446, f 8, 27 July 1841

Chapter 2 DOMESTIC POLICY: FINANCIAL AND SOCIAL
(pages 45-78)

1   Gash, *Peel*, 298

2 For Stanley's opinions, see Peel Papers, 40467, ff 42-9, Stanley to Peel, 7 Aug 1841; for Graham's opinions, see Peel Papers, 40446, ff 9-16, Graham to Peel, 1 Aug 1841, and Peel Papers, 40446, f 184 Graham to Peel, 12 Dec 1841

3 Peel Papers, 40444, ff 1-4, Goulburn to Peel, 22 July 1841

4 Ibid, 40464, ff 31-2, Ripon to Peel, 7 Oct 1841

5 Ibid, 40446, ff 181-4, Graham to Peel, 12 Dec 1841

6 Graham Papers, Bundle 7 Ir, Graham to de Grey, 3 Feb 1842

7 *Hansard*, LX, 231, 9 Feb 1842

8 Ibid, 235, 9 Feb 1842

9 Ibid, LXI, 430-31, 11 March 1842

10 Ibid, 466

11 Ibid, LXII, 323-4, 12 April 1842

12 Ibid, LXIII, 662, 23 May 1842

13 Gash, *Peel*, 326

14 *Hansard*, LXIX, 620, 19 May 1843

15 Ibid, 971, 26 May 1843

16 Ibid, LXXIV, 363, 29 April 1844

17 Ibid, 380. There were also reductions on stamp duties used in marine insurances, and the abolition of the wool duty. For a brief discussion of the budget of 1844, see Gash, *Peel*, 430-1

18 Parker, *Peel*, III, 170, 18 Feb 1845

19 *Hansard*, LXXVII, 599, 17 Feb 1845

20 Ibid, 627

21 Ibid, LXXVIII, 1038, 17 March 1845

22 Parker, *Peel*, III, 172, 22 March 1845

23 Peel Papers, 40470, ff 94 ff, memo by Goulburn, undated

24 *Hansard*, LXIII, 1214, 3 June 1842

25 Ibid, LXX, 227, 232, 22 June 1843

26 This was Stafford O'Brien, MP for North Northamptonshire; *Hansard*, LXXV, 1077, 17 June 1844

27 Graham Papers, Bundle 20 Ir, Graham to Heytesbury, 19 Feb 1845

28 *Hansard*, LXXVII, 1235, 26 Feb 1845

29 Ibid, 1288-1306, 26 Feb 1845 for Macaulay's speech

30 Ibid, 1269, 26 Feb 1845. Decades later, Gladstone could afford to be more candid about the weakness of the ministry's sugar policy. Conceding the opposition's more consistent case, he also admitted (in an unconsciously appropriate phrase) the 'complex and over-refined' policy of the ministry (Brooke, John, and Sorensen, Mary (eds). *The Prime Ministers' Papers: W. E. Gladstone*, (London, 1972), I, 61-2, from a memorandum written by Gladstone in 1897)

31 *Hansard*, LXXVII, 1309, 26 Feb 1845

32 Roseveare, Henry. *The Treasury: The Evolution of a British Institution* (London, 1969), 186-7

33 Checkland, S. G. *The Rise of Industrial Society in England, 1815-1885* (London, 1964), 13-14

34 *Hansard*, LXXVI, 275, 3 July 1844

35 Hunt, Bishop Carleton. *The Development of the Business Corpora-
    tion in England, 1800-1867* (Cambridge, Mass, 1936), 94. For a gen-
    eral discussion of the bill, see Hunt, *Business Corporation in England*,
    chap 5; and Hyde, Francis Edwin. *Mr. Gladstone at the Board of
    Trade* (London, 1935), chap 8
36 See Pressnell, L. S. *Country Banking in the Industrial Revolution
    (Clarendon Press, 1956), chap 16*
37 Horsefield, J. K. 'The Origins of the Bank Charter Act, 1844'
    Economica, New Series, Vol XI, No 44 (Nov 1944), 180; Clapham,
    Sir John. *The Bank of England: A History*. (Cambridge and New
    York, 1945), II, 177
38 *Hansard*, LXI, 140, 7 March 1842
39 Ibid, LIX, 941-2, 28 Sept 1841
40 Ibid, LXV, 508-9, 22 July 1842
41 Ibid, LXIII, 1358, 7 June 1842
42 Ibid, LXV, 7, 116-7, 120-2, 12 July 1842
43 Ibid, 1098, 6 Aug 1842
44 Ibid, LXVIII, 1439, 24 March 1843
45 Graham Papers, Bundle 52B, Graham to Shuttleworth, 30 Aug 1842
46 Parker, Charles Stuart (ed). *Life and Letters of Sir James Graham*
    (London, 1901), I, 344
47 *Hansard*, LXVII, 1417, 24 March 1843
48 Ibid, 1419, 24 March 1843
49 Perkin, Harold. *The Origins of Modern English Society, 1780-1880*
    (London, 1969), 352
50 *Hansard*, LXXIII, 1247, 18 March 1844
51 Brooke and Sorensen, *Prime Ministers' Papers, Gladstone*, II, 254
52 *Hansard*, LXXIII, 1489-90, 25 March 1844
53 Brooke and Sorensen, *Prime Ministers' Papers, Gladstone*, II, 254
54 *Hansard*, LXXIV, 916, 10 May 1844
55 Ibid, 952, 10 May 1844
56 Stewart, Robert. 'The Ten Hours and Sugar Crises of 1844: Govern-
    ment and the House of Commons in the Age of Reform', *Historical
    Journal*, Vol XII, No 1 (1969), 54
57 *Hansard*, LXXVII, 658, 18 Feb 1845
58 *The Times*, 11 Nov 1842
59 *Hansard*, LXIV, 179, 18 June 1842
60 Ibid, LXXVI, 489, 8 July 1844
61 See the notes from Peel, Stanley, Graham, and Goulburn in Glad-
    stone Papers, Add Ms 44650, ff 202-5, during May and June 1844.
    Peel thought the provisions would be 'a precedent dangerous to the
    security of all property' (ibid, f 202, 18 May 1844)
62 Gladstone's speech is contained in the short discussion found in
    Hansard, LXXVI, 1185-91, 22 July 1844
63 Cleveland-Stevens, Edward. *English Railways: Their Development
    and their Relation to the State* (London, 1915), 25

64   *Hansard*, LXXVII, 179, 6 Feb 1845
65   Ibid, 148, 5 Feb 1845
66   There were 145 railway directors among the members of this parliament (estimated by Aydelotte, W. O. 'The House of Commons in the 1840s', *History*, New Series, Vol XXXIX, No 137 (Oct 1954), 249-62)
67   The best-known empiricist is Oliver MacDonagh. See his seminal articles 'Emigration and the State, 1833-55: An Essay in Administrative History', *Transactions of the Royal Historical Society*, 5th Series, Vol V (1955), 133-59, and 'The Nineteenth Century Revolution in Government: A Reappraisal'. *Historical Journal*, Vol I, No 1 (1958), 52-67; and his book *A Pattern of Government Growth, 1800-1860: The Passenger Acts and their Enforcement* (London, 1961). Theorists include Parris, Henry, 'The Nineteenth Century Revolution in Government: a Reappraisal Reappraised', *Historical Journal*, Vol II, No 1 (1960), 17-37; and Finer, S. E. 'The Transmission of Benthamite Ideas, 1820-50' in Sutherland, Gillian (ed). *Studies in the Growth of Nineteenth Century Government* (London, 1972), 11-32. A summary of the debate may be found in Cromwell, Valerie, 'Interpretations of Nineteenth Century Administration: An Analysis', *Victorian Studies*, Vol IX, No 3, (March 1966), 245-55

Chapter 3 IRELAND: CLOUD IN THE WEST (pages 79-101)

1   *The Times*, 28 March 1842
2   *The Pilot*, 15 May 1843
3   *The Pilot*, 24 Feb 1843
4   Ibid, 13 Feb 1843
5   Ibid, 26 April 1843
6   Ibid, 19 April 1843
7   For this debate, see *Hansard*, LX, 1400-29, 3 March 1842
8   Ibid, 1424, 3 March 1842
9   Lee, Joseph. 'The Provision of Capital for Early Irish Railways, 1830-53', *Irish Historical Studies*, Vol XVI, No 61 (March 1968), 55
10   According to Gladstone's memorandum of the meeting, Brooke and Sorensen, *Prime Ministers' Papers: Gladstone*, II, 204-5
11   This is Professor Gash's view: see his *Peel*, 395
12   *Hansard*, LXIX, 25, 9 May 1843
13   Graham Papers, Bundle 61A, 21 May 1843
14   *The Pilot*, 14 June 1843
15   Graham Papers, Bundle 62A, 2 June 1843
16   In July, Graham sent to Ireland a shorthand writer to make verbatim reports of repeal speeches (Graham Papers, Bundle 63, Graham to de Grey, 1 July 1843)
17   *The Pilot*, 16 Aug 1843
18   Ibid, 13 Sept 1843

19   For the Clifden meeting, see *The Pilot*, 20 Sept 1843
20   *Freeman's Journal*, 30 Sept 1843
21   Graham Papers, Bundle 71A, Graham to de Grey, 1 March 1844
22   *Hansard*, LXX, 643-4, 4 July 1843. For a similar complaint, see the speech of Sir H. W. Barron (Waterford City) in ibid, 118, 19 June 1843
23   Parker, *Peel*, III, 22 Aug 1843, 57
24   Peel Papers, 40478, ff 150-1, 18 Aug 1843
25   *Dublin Evening Mail*, 1 Sept 1843
26   See the exchange of letters between Eliot and Peel in Peel Papers, 40480, ff 118-19, 23 Sept 1842; ff 120-3, 27 Sept 1842; ff 132-5, 12 Oct 1842; ff 145-8, 13 Nov 1842
27   Parker, *Peel*, III, 20 Oct 1843, 65
28   See Gladstone's account of the cabinet meetings of 11 and 13 February in Brooke and Sorensen, *Prime Ministers' Papers: Gladstone*, II, 230-4
29   *Report from Her Majesty's Commissioners of Inquiry into the State of the Law and Practice in Respect to the Occupation of Land in Ireland* (1845), XIX-XX
30   For the debate on the second reading, from which these quotations were taken, see *Hansard*, LXXXI, 1117-52, 24 June 1845; for Stanley's introduction of the bill, see *Hansard* LXXXI, 211-35, 9 June 1845
31   Peel Papers, 40479, f 288, 9 Feb 1845
32   Ibid, 40445, f 5, 6 Jan 1845
33   As he put it in a letter to the Queen: Parker, *Peel*, III, 9 April 1845, 173
34   *Hansard*, LXXIX, 23, 3 April 1845
35   *The Times*, 16 April 1845, 14 April 1845, 3 April 1845
36   *Hansard*, LXXIX, 42, 3 April 1845
37   Ibid, 916, 17 April 1845
38   Ibid, 887
39   Ibid, 555-69, 11 April 1845, for Disraeli's speech
40   Ibid, 90, 3 April 1845
41   Gash, *Peel*, 477
42   *Hansard*, LXXIX, 773-4, 16 April 1845
43   These extracts were taken from the Graham Papers, Bundle 88, 4 April 1845, 12 April 1845, and 23 April 1845
44   Parker, *Peel*, III, ff 118-19, Heytesbury to Peel, 8 Aug 1844
45   *Hansard*, LXXX, 378, 9 May 1845
46   Basset, A. Tilney (ed). *Gladstone to his Wife* (London, 1936), letter dated 12 Oct 1845, 64

Chapter 4 RELUCTANT IMPERALISTS (pages 102-137)

1   Furley, Oliver. 'The Humanitarian Impact', in Bartlett, C.J. (ed). *Britain Pre-Eminent: Studies of British World Influence in the Nineteenth Century* (London, 1969), 130

2   Aberdeen Papers, 43061, ff 317-20, Peel to Aberdeen, 1 Nov 1841
3   *Hansard*, LXXXII, 63, 7 July 1845. See also Jones, Wilbur Dever-
    eux. 'The Origins and Passage of Lord Aberdeen's Act', *Hispanic-
    American Historical Review*, Vol XLII, No 4 (Nov 1962), 502-20
4   Aberdeen Papers, 43064, f 53, 18 Oct 1844
5   Peel Papers, 40453, ff 30-1, Peel to Aberdeen, 17 Oct 1841
6   *Hansard*, LXXVI, 1575, 31 July 1844
7   For this cabinet discussion, see Peel Papers, 40460, ff 254-5, 16 Aug
    1844; 40454, ff 238-40, 28 Aug 1844; 40450, f 116, 23 Aug 1844;
    40454, f 216, 19 Aug 1844; Aberdeen Papers, 43063, ff 324-30, 21
    Aug 1844
8   For the following discussion, see Gash, *Peel*, 517-25; and Bartlett,
    C.J. *Great Britain and Sea Power, 1815-1853* (Oxford, 1963), 148-74
9   Peel Papers, 40454, ff 225-6, 21 Aug 1844
10 Bourne, Kenneth. *Britain and the Balance of Power in North
    America, 1815-1908* (London, 1967), 93-5, esp 94 n2
11 *The Times*, 17 Sept 1842
12 See the debate in *Hansard*, LXVII, 1162-1285, 21 March 1843
13 Russell Papers, PRO 30/22/4C, 24 Sept 1842
14 Peel Papers, 40468, f 209, 5 Sept 1844
15 Ibid, ff 211 ff, 7 Sept 1844
16 Peel Papers, 40455, ff 172-3, 23 Sept 1845. Previous historians, as
    Bourne has noted (*Britain and the Balance of Power in North
    America*, 122, esp n1) have tended to minimise unduly the British
    government's interest in California
17 Peel Papers, 40455, ff 176-8, 23 Sept 1845: see also the brief discus-
    sion in Jones, *Aberdeen and the Americas*, 68-71
18 For the Oregon debate, see *Hansard*, LXXIX, 178-201, 4 April 1845
19 Ibid, 123, 4 April 1845
20 See his letter to Aberdeen in Aberdeen Papers, 43062, ff 48-54, 16
    May 1842; and to Stanley, Peel Papers, 40468, ff 124 ff, 2 Feb 1844
21 Fairbank, John King. *Trade and Diplomacy on the China Coast: The
    Opening of the Treaty Ports, 1842-1854* (Cambridge, Mass, 1953),
    66
22 Greenberg, Michael, *British Trade and the Opening of China, 1800-
    42* (Cambridge, 1951) 105, 221
23 See, for example, leaders in *The Times* of 8 Feb 1842, 4 Aug 1842, and
    14 Nov 1842
24 Brook and Sorensen, *Prime Ministers' Papers: Gladstone*, II, 156-67
25 Peel Papers, 40453, f 291, Peel to Aberdeen, 22 Dec 1842
26 Ellenborough Papers, PRO 30/12/68, despatch of Stanley to Ellen-
    borough, 31 Dec 1841
27 Aberdeen Papers, 43072, ff 25-6, 15 Oct 1842
28 Ibid, ff 27-30, 17 Oct 1842
29 Aberdeen Papers, 43127, 8 Oct 1845, quoted in Jones, *Aberdeen and
    the Americas*, 50
30 Aberdeen Papers, 43065, ff 127-8, 28 Dec 1845

31 Ibid, 40455, ff 290-1, 28 Dec 1845
32 For this early statement of Gladstone's anti-imperial views, see FO
    12/4/127-34, dated 18 June 1846
33 Ibid
34 FO 12/4/142-58, dated 25 June 1846
35 FO 12/4, f 132, 18 June 1846, Gladstone to Aberdeen
36 Semmel, Bernard. 'The Philosophical Radicals and Colonialism', in
    Shaw, A. G. L. (ed). *Great Britain and the Colonies, 1815-1865* (London, 1970), 79
37 Morrell, W. P. *British Colonial Policy in the Age of Peel and Russell*
    (Oxford, 1930), 119
38 *Hansard*, LXXXI, 676, 17 June 1845
39 Ibid, LXXXII, 1007, 23 July 1845
40 As a report to *The Times* put it, 9 March 1842
41 Brooke and Sorensen, *Prime Ministers' Papers: Gladstone*, II, 203
42 *The Times*, 5 May 1843
43 *Hansard*, LXVII, 702, 9 March 1843
44 Huttenback, Robert A. *British Relations with Sind, 1799-1843: An
    Anatomy of Imperialism* (Berkeley, 1962), 114
45 Peel Papers, 40471, f 305, Ellenborough to Peel, 20 May 1843
46 Ellenborough Papers, PRO 30/12/1/6, ff 543-6, 24 March 1843
47 The phrase is Peel's as reported by Gladstone in his cabinet memo-
    randum of 22 Nov 1843, cited in Brooke and Sorensen, *Prime Minis-
    ters' Papers: Gladstone*, II, 226. See also ibid, 202 and 208-12, for
    cabinet opinion on the Scinde question
48 Peel Papers, 40462, ff 12-16, 4 Sept 1841. The memorandum was
    sent to Aberdeen
49 As reported by Gladstone, cited in Brooke and Sorensen, *Prime
    Ministers' Papers: Gladstone*, II, 257
50 Parker, *Peel*, III, 18 Aug 1845, Hardinge to Peel, 274; 6 Nov 1844,
    Peel to Hardinge, 264
51 Gallagher, John, and Robinson, Ronald. 'The Imperialism of Free
    Trade', *Economic History Review*, 2nd Series, Vol VI, No 1 (1953),
    1-15
52 Mathew, W. M. 'The Imperialism of Free Trade: Peru, 1820-70',
    Economic History Review, 2nd Series, Vol XXI, No 3 (1968)
53 MacDonagh, Oliver. 'The Anti-Imperialism of Free Trade', *Economic
    History Review*, 2nd Series, Vol XIV, No 3 (1962), 489-501
54 Platt, D. C. M. 'The Imperialism of Free Trade: Some Reservations',
    Economic History Review, 2nd Series, Vol XXI, No 2 (1968), 296-
    306
55 MacDonagh, 'Anti-Imperialism of Free Trade', 500

Chapter 5 THE END OF THE MINISTRY (pages 138-156)

 1 *Hansard*, LXXX, 740, 21 May 1845. Peel made these remarks in his
    justification of the increased grant to Maynooth

2   Peel Papers, 40472, f 104, Peel to Ellenborough, 1 Nov 1843
3   Graham Papers, Bundle 95A, Peel to Graham, 11 Nov 1845
4   Peel Papers, 40468, f 383, Stanley to Peel, 3 Nov 1845
5   Derby Ms, 27/5, cabinet memorandum, 3 Nov 1845
6   Peel Papers, 40481, ff 322-31, Lincoln to Peel, 5 Nov 1845
7   Ibid, 40455, ff 276-8, Goulburn to Peel, 27 Nov 1845
8   Russell Papers, PRO 30/22/4D, f 282, Palmerston to Russell, 21 Oct 1845
9   Grey was better known as Lord Howick. He had recently succeeded as the third Earl on the death of his father
10 Russell Papers, PRO 30/22/4E, ff 219-21, 19 Dec 1845. Some confirmation of this came from Paris that very week. Henry Reeve reported to Russell that 'The name of Palmerston sent down the funds more than a franc on Saturday morning . . .' (Russell Papers, PRO 30/22/4E, f 165, 15 Dec 1845)
11 Peel Papers, 40461, f 355, Wellington memorandum, 30 Nov 1845
12 Russell Papers, PRO 30/22/5A, f 44, Palmerston to Russell, 5 Jan 1846
13 Ellenborough Papers, PRO 30/12/21/7, f 333, Redesdale to Ellenborough, 28 Dec 1845
14 Peel Papers, 40461, f 388, Rutland to Wellington, 12 Jan 1846
15 Derby Ms, 132/13, Bentinck to Stanley, 7 Jan 1846
16 *Lincolnshire Chronicle*, 9 Jan 1846
17 Ibid, 26 Dec 1845
18 Ibid, 19 Dec 1845
19 *Essex Standard*, 12 Dec 1845
20 Ibid, 16 Jan 1846
21 *Cornwall Royal Gazette*, 19 Dec 1845
22 For Fremantle's letter to Graham, see Graham Papers, Bundle 98, 5 Jan 1846: for Graham's letter to Heytesbury, ibid, Bundle 99, 3 Feb 1846
23 Peel Papers, 40585, f 142, 18 Feb 1846. For a discussion of the Peelite by-election fortunes, see Jones, William Devereux, and Erickson, Arvel B. *The Peelites, 1846-1857* (Ohio State, 1972), chap 4
24 Parker, *Peel*, III, Peel to the Right Hon William Peel, 31 Jan 1846, 337
25 *Hansard*, LXXXIII, 594, 9 Feb 1846: speech of A. J. B. Hope (Maidstone)
26 Ibid, 23, 22 Jan 1846
27 Ibid, 239, 27 Jan 1846
28 Ibid, 74, 22 Jan 1846
29 Ibid, 258-9, 27 Jan 1846
30 Peel Papers, 40580, ff 205-7, Peel to Sir Francis Egerton, 11 Dec 1845
31 *Hansard*, LXXXIII, 328, 27 Jan 1846
32 Ibid, 1003, 16 Feb 1846
33 Ibid, 593, 9 Feb 1846

34 Ibid, LXXXIV, 349, 27 Feb 1846
35 Ibid, LXXXVI, 675-6, 15 May 1846
36 Ibid, LXXXVII, 182, 8 June 1846
37 Graham Papers, Bundle 102, 11 June 1846
38 Gash, *Peel*, 606
39 *Hansard*, LXXXVII, 1026-7, 25 June 1846

EPILOGUE (pages 157-160)

1 Parker, *Peel*, III, Peel to Hardinge, 24 Sept 1846, 474
2 Ibid, Graham to Peel, 8 Dec 1849, 525
3 There are different interpretations of this episode between Gash, *Peel*, 627-31, and Prest, *Russell*, 265-7. To this author, Gash's is the more convincing
4 Parker, *Peel*, III, 513-16
5 Conacher, J. B. 'Peel and the Peelites, 1846-1850', *English Historical Review*, Vol LXXIII (July 1958), 431

Appendix

Peel's Cabinet, 1841-1846
[Reproduced from Woodward, Sir Llewellyn. *The Age of Reform,
1815-1870* (Oxford, Clarendon Press, 1962), 662-3]
Prime Minister and First Lord of the Treasury: Sir R. Peel
Lord Chancellor: Lord Lyndhurst
Lord President of the Council: Lord Wharncliffe
Lord Privy Seal: Duke of Buckingham
Chancellor of the Exchequer: H. Goulburn
Home Secretary: Sir James Graham
Foreign Secretary: Earl of Aberdeen
Secretary of War and Colonies: Viscount Stanley
First Lord of the Admiralty: Earl of Haddington
President of the Board of Trade: Earl of Ripon
President of the Board of Control: Lord Ellenborough
(created earl 1844)
Secretary at War: Sir H. Hardinge
Paymaster-General: Sir E. Knatchbull
Cabinet minister without office: Duke of Wellington

Changes

October 1841: Lord Fitzgerald (formerly W. Vesey-Fitzgerald)
entered the cabinet as President of the Board of Control on Lord
Ellenborough's appointment as Governor-General of India. January 1842: the Duke of Buckingham resigned and the Duke of
Buccleuch took his place as lord Privy Seal. May 1843: the Earl
of Ripon succeeded Lord Fitzgerald as President of the Board
of Control; his successor as President of the Board of Trade was
W. E. Gladstone. May 1844: Lord Granville Somerset entered the
cabinet as Chancellor of the Duchy of Lancaster; Sir H. Hardinge
was appointed Governor-General of India; his successor as Secretary at War was not in the cabinet. January and February 1845:
W. E. Gladstone (January) and Sir E. Knatchbull (February) re-

signed; their successors were not in the cabinet; the Earl of Lincoln joined the cabinet (January) as First Commissioner of Woods and Forests. May 1845: S. Herbert joined the cabinet as Secretary at War.

Bibliography

MANUSCRIPT COLLECTIONS

British Museum Additional Manuscripts
  Aberdeen Papers
  Gladstone Papers
  Peel Papers
Cambridge University Library
  Graham Papers
Hughenden, High Wycombe
  Hughenden Papers
Public Record Office, London
  Ellenborough Papers
  Foreign Office Papers
  Russell Papers
Queen's College, Oxford
  Derby Papers

PARLIAMENTARY PUBLICATIONS

Hansard's Parliamentary Debates, 3rd Series
1842, V, *Report from the Select Committee on Election Proceedings*
1845, XIX-XX, *Report from Her Majesty's Commissioners of Inquiry into the State of the Law and Practice in Respect to the Occupation of Land in Ireland*

POLL BOOKS

Bristol Poll Book (Bristol, 1841)
The Poll . . . Cambridge (1841)

Poll Book . . . for the Borough of Liverpool 1841 (Liverpool, 1841)

An Alphabetical Copy of the Poll . . . of . . . the Borough of Newcastle-under-Lyme (Newcastle-under-Lyme, 1841)

Northampton Borough Election [1841]

An Alphabetical List of the Burgesses, Occupiers, and Freeholders who polled at the election of a Burgess to Represent the Town of Nottingham . . . April 1841 (Nottingham, 1841)

A Correct List of the Voters . . . for the Borough of Reading (Reading, 1841)

PERIODICALS AND NEWSPAPERS

Annual Register
Berkshire Chronicle
Birmingham Journal
Bristol Gazette
Bucks Herald
Cambridge Chronicle
Carlisle Patriot
Cornwall Royal Gazette
Dublin Evening Mail
Essex Standard
Freeman's Journal
Ipswich Express
Ispwich Journal
Leeds Mercury
Leicester Journal
Leicester Mercury
Lincolnshire Chronicle
Liverpool Courier
Manchester Guardian
Morning Chronicle
Newcastle Chronicle
Norfolk Chronicle
Northampton Herald
Northampton Mercury
North Staffordshire Advertiser

Northern Star
Norwich Mercury
Nottingham Mercury
Nottingham Review
The Pilot
Staffordshire Advertiser
The Times
York Herald
Yorkshire Gazette

SECONDARY WORKS

Adams, E. D. *British Interests and Activities in Texas, 1838-1846* (Baltimore, 1910)

Adamson, John William. *English Education, 1789-1902* (Cambridge, 1930)

Akenson, Donald H. *The Irish Education Experiment: The National System of Education in the Nineteenth Century* (London and Toronto, 1970)

Andréadès, A. *History of the Bank of England, 1640 to 1903,* 4th ed (London reprint, 1966)

Balfour, Lady Frances. *Life of the Fourth Earl of Aberdeen,* Vol II (London, 1923)

Bartlett, C. J. *Great Britain and Sea Power, 1815-1853* (Oxford, 1963)

Basset, A. Tilney (ed). *Gladstone to his Wife* (London, 1936)

Black, R. D. Collison. *Economic Thought and the Irish Question, 1817-1870* (Cambridge, 1960)

Blake, Robert. *The Conservative Party from Peel to Churchill* (New York, 1970)

Blakiston, Georgiana. *Lord William Russell and his Wife, 1815-1846* (London, 1972)

Bloomfield, Paul. *Edward Gibbon Wakefield: Builder of the British Commonwealth* (London, 1961)

Bourne, Kenneth. *Britain and the Balance of Power in North America, 1815-1908* (London, 1967)

Boyson, Rhodes. *The Ashworth Cotton Enterprise: the Rise and Fall of a Family Firm, 1818-1880* (Oxford, 1970)

Brown, Lucy. *The Board of Trade and the Free Trade Movement, 1830-1842* (Oxford, 1958)

Cady, John F. *Foreign Intervention in the Rio de la Plata, 1838-50* (Philadelphia and London, 1929)

Checkland, S. G. *The Rise of Industrial Society in England, 1815-1885* (London, 1964)

Church, Roy A. *Economic and Social Change in a Midland Town: Victorian Nottingham, 1815-1900* (London reprint, 1966)

Clapham, Sir John. *The Bank of England: A History,* Vol II (Cambridge and New York, 1945)

Cleveland-Stevens, Edward. *English Railways: Their Development and their Relation to the State* (London, 1915)

Colchester, Lord (ed). *History of the Indian Administration of Lord Ellenborough* (London, 1874)

Cullen, L. M. *An Economic History of Ireland since 1660* (London, 1972)

Davis, Richard W. *Political Change and Continuity, 1760-1885: A Buckinghamshire Study* (Newton Abbot, 1972)

Driver, Cecil. *Tory Radical: The Life of Richard Oastler (New York, 1946)*

Fairbank, John King, *Trade and Diplomacy on the China Coast: The Opening of the Treaty Ports, 1842-1854* (Cambridge, Mass, 1953)

Ferns, H. S. *Britain and Argentina in the Nineteenth Century* (Oxford, 1960)

Flinn, M. W. (ed). *Edwin Chadwick's Report on the Sanitary Condition of the Labouring Population of Great Britain* (Edinburgh, 1965)

Flournoy, Francis Rosebro. *British Policy towards Morocco in the Age of Palmerston, 1830-1865* (Baltimore and London, 1935)

Galbraith, John S. *The Hudson's Bay Company as an Imperial Factor, 1821-1869* (Berkeley and Los Angeles, 1957)

——. *Reluctant Empire: British Policy on the South African Frontier, 1834-1854* (Berkeley and Los Angeles, 1963)

Gash, Norman. *Politics in the Age of Peel* (London, 1953)

——. *Mr. Secretary Peel: The Life of Sir Robert Peel to 1830* (London and Cambridge, Mass, 1961)

——. *Reaction and Reconstruction in English Politics, 1832-1852* (Oxford, 1965)

_____. *Sir Robert Peel: The Life of Sir Robert Peel after 1830* (London and Towata, NJ, 1972)

Gladstone, W. E., *The Prime Ministers' Papers*. ed John Brooke and Mary Sorensen, Vol II (London, 1972)

Graham, Life and Letters of Sir James. ed Charles Stuart Parker, Vol I (London, 1901)

Greenberg, Michael. *British Trade and the Opening of China, 1800-42* (Cambridge, 1951)

Greville Memoirs. ed Henry Reeve, Vol I (New York, 1885)

Hall, John. *England and the Orleans Monarchy* (London, 1912)

Hamburger, Joseph. *James Mill and the Art of Revolution* (New Haven and London, 1963)

Hammond, J. L., and Foot, M. R. D. *Gladstone and Liberalism* (New York, Collier Paperback, 1966)

Hobsbawm, E. J. *Labouring Men* (London, 1964)

Hodder, Edwin. *The Life and Work of the Seventh Earl of Shaftesbury, K. G.*, Vol I (London, 1886)

Hunt, Bishop Carleton. *The Development of the Business Corporation in England, 1800-1867* (Cambridge, Mass, 1936)

Huttenback, Robert A. *British Relations with Sind, 1799-1843: An Anatomy of Imperialism* (Berkeley, 1962)

Hyde, Francis Edwin. *Mr. Gladstone at the Board of Trade* (London, 1935)

Imlah, Albert H. *Lord Ellenborough, A Biography of Edward Law, Earl of Ellenborough, Governor-General of India* (Cambridge, Mass, 1939)

Jones, Kathleen. *A History of the Mental Health Service* (London and Boston, 1972)

Jones, Wilbur Devereux. *Lord Aberdeen and the Americas* (Athens, Ga, 1958)

_____. *'Prosperity' Robinson: the Life of Viscount Goderich, 1782-1859* (New York, 1967)

_____. and Erickson, Arvel B. *The Peelites, 1846-1857* (Ohio State, 1972)

Knaplund, Paul Alexander. *James Stephen and the British Colonial System* (Madison, Wis, 1953)

Lieven–Palmerston Correspondence, 1828-1856. ed. Lord Sudley (London, 1943)

MacDonagh, Oliver. *A Pattern of Government Growth, 1800-1860:
The Passenger Acts and their Enforcement* (London, 1961)

McDowell, R. B. *Public Opinion and Government Policy in
Ireland, 1801-1846* (London, 1952)

Manchester, Alan K. *British Preeminence in Brazil: Its Rise and
Decline* (New York reprint, 1972)

Manning, Bernard Lord. *The Protestant Dissenting Deputies*
(Cambridge, 1952)

Mather, F. C. *Public Order in the Age of the Chartists* (Manchester,
1959)

Matthews, R. C. O. *A Study in Trade-Cycle History: Economic
Fluctuations in Great Britain, 1833-1842* (Cambridge, 1954)

Merk, Frederick. *The Monroe Doctrine and American Expansion-
ism, 1843-1849* (New York, 1966)

——. *The Oregon Question: Essays in Anglo-American Diplomacy and Politics* (Cambridge, Mass, 1967)

Miller, John. *Early Victorian New Zealand: A Study of Racial
Tension and Social Attitudes, 1839-1852* (London, 1958)

Moody, T. W., and Becket, J. C. *Queen's Belfast 1845-1949: The
Story of a University*, Vol I (London, 1959)

Morley, John. *The Life of William Ewart Gladstone*, Vol I (London, 1903)

Morrell, W. P. *British Colonial Policy in the Age of Peel and
Russell* (Oxford, 1930)

——. *Britain in the Pacific Islands* (Oxford, 1960)

Neale, R. S. *Class and Ideology in the Nineteenth Century* (London
and Boston, 1972)

Nicholls, Sir George. *A History of the English Poor Law*, new
ed, Vol II (New York reprint, 1967)

Norris, J. A. *The First Afghan War, 1838-1842* (Cambridge, 1967)

O'Connell, Daniel, Correspondence of. ed W. J. Fitzpatrick, Vol
II (London, 1888)

Overstone, Lord, Correspondence of. ed D. P. O'Brien, Vol I
(Cambridge, 1971)

Parris, Henry. *Government and the Railways in Nineteenth-
Century Britain* (London and Toronto, 1965)

Parry, E. Jones. *The Spanish Marriages, 1841-1846: A Study of the
Influence of Dynastic Ambition upon Foreign Policy* (London
1936)

Patterson, A. Temple. *Radical Leicester: A History of Leicester, 1780-1850* (Leicester, 1954),

Peel, Sir Robert. ed Charles Stuart Parker, Vol II (London, 1899)

Perkin, Harold. *The Origins of Modern English Society, 1780-1880* (London, 1969)

Pollard, Sidney. *A History of Labour in Sheffield* (Liverpool, 1959)

Pressnell, L. S. *Country Banking in the Industrial Revolution* (Oxford, 1956)

Prest, John. *Lord John Russell* (London, 1972)

Redford, Arthur. *Manchester Merchants and Foreign Trade, 1794-1858* (Manchester, 1934)

Roberts, David. *Victorian Origins of the British Welfare State* (New Haven, 1968)

Roseveare, Henry. *The Treasury: The Evolution of a British Institution* (London, 1969)

Runciman, Steven. *The White Rajahs: A History of Sarawak from 1841 to 1946* (Cambridge, 1960)

Sayers, R. S. *Lloyds Bank in the History of English Banking* (Oxford, 1957)

Schoyen, A. R. *The Chartist Challenge: A Portrait of George Julian Harney* (New York, 1958)

Smith, Frank. *The Life and Work of Sir James Kay-Shuttleworth* (London, 1923)

Spring, David. *The English Landed Estate: Its Administration* (Baltimore, 1963)

Temperley, Howard. *British Anti-Slavery, 1833-1870* (London, 1972)

Thomas, Maurice Walton. *The Early Factory Legislation: A Study in Legislative and Administrative Evolution* (Leigh on Sea, 1948)

Thomis, Malcolm I. *Politics and Society in Nottingham, 1785-1835* (New York, 1969)

Vincent, J. R. *Pollbooks: How Victorians Voted* (Cambridge, 1967)

Ward, John M. *British Policy in the South Pacific (1786-1893)* (Sydney, 1948)

Ward, John Towers. *The Factory Movement, 1830-1855* (London and New York, 1962)

Ward, John Trevor. *Sir James Graham* (London, 1967)
Webster, Sir Charles. *The Foreign Policy of Palmerston, 1830-1841* (London, 1951)
Williams, Judith Blow. *British Commercial Policy and Trade Expansion, 1750-1850* (Oxford, 1972)
Wrong, E. M. *Charles Buller and Responsible Government* (Oxford, 1926)
Wyncoll, Peter. *Nottingham Chartism* (Nottingham, 1966)

ARTICLES

Aydellotte, W. O. 'The Country Gentlemen and the Repeal of the Corn Laws', *English Historical Review*, Vol LXXXII (Jan 1967), 47-60
Beer, Samuel H. 'The Representation of Interests in British Government: Historical Background', *American Political Science Review*, Vol LI, No 3 (Sept 1957), 613-50
Conacher, J. B. 'Peel and the Peelites, 1846-1850', *English Historical Review*, Vol LXXIII (July 1958), 431-52
Cromwell, Valerie. 'Interpretations of Nineteenth Century Administration: An Analysis', *Victorian Studies*, Vol IX, No 3 (March 1966), 245-55
Finer, S. E. 'The Transmission of Benthamite Ideas, 1820-50', in *Studies in the Growth of Nineteenth Century Government*, ed Gillian Sutherland (London, 1972)
Fraser, Peter. 'Public Petitioning and Parliament before 1832', *History*, Vol XLVI, No 158 (Oct 1961), 195-211
Furley, Oliver. 'The Humanitarian Impact', in *Britain Pre-Eminent: Studies of British World Influence in the Nineteenth Century*, ed C. J. Bartlett (London, 1969)
Gallagher, John, and Robinson, Ronald. 'The Imperialism of Free Trade', *Economic History Review*, 2nd Series, Vol VI, No 1 (1953), 1-15
Hanham, H. J. 'Ashburton as a Parliamentary Borough', *Devonshire Association for the Advancement of Science, Literature and Art, Report and Transactions*, Vol XCVIII (1966), 206-56

Horsefield, J. K. 'The Origins of the Bank Charter Act, 1844', *Economica*, New Series, Vol XI, No 44 (Nov 1944), 180-9

Jones, Wilbur Devereux. 'The Origins and Passage of Lord Aberdeen's Act', *Hispanic American Historical Review*, Vol XLII, No 4 (Nov 1962), 502-20

Lee, Joseph. 'The Provision of Capital for Early Irish Railways, 1830-53', *Irish Historical Studies*, Vol XVI, No 61 (March 1968), 33-63

Lucas, B. Keith. 'County Meetings', *Law Quarterly Review*, Vol LXX (Jan 1954), 109-14

MacDonagh, Oliver. 'Emigration and the State, 1833-55: An Essay in Administrative History', *Transactions of the Royal Historical Society*, 5th Series, Vol V (1955), 133-59

———. 'The Nineteenth Century Revolution in Government: A Reappraisal', *Historical Journal*, Vol I, No 1 (1958), 52-67

———. 'The Anti-Imperialism of Free Trade', *Economic History Review*, 2nd Series, Vol XIV, No 3 (1962), 489-501

Mathew, W. M. 'The Imperialism of Free Trade: Peru, 1820-70', *Economic History Review*, 2nd Series, Vol XXI, No 3 (1968), 562-79

Nossiter, T. J. 'Shopkeeper Radicalism in the 19th Century', in *Imagination and Precision in the Social Sciences*, ed T. J. Nossiter, A. H. Hanson and Stein Rokkan (London, 1972)

Parris, Henry. 'The Nineteenth Century Revolution in Government: A Reappraisal Reappraised', *Historical Journal*, Vol III, No 1 (1960), 17-37

Peacock, A. J. 'Bradford Chartism, 1838-1840', *Borthwick Papers*, No 36 (York, 1969)

Platt, D. C. M. 'The Imperialism of Free Trade: Some Reservations', *Economic History Review*, 2nd Series, Vol XXI, No 2 (1968), 296-306

Semmel, Bernard. 'The Philosophical Radicals and Colonialism', in *Great Britain and the Colonies, 1815-1865*, ed A. G. L. Shaw (London, 1970)

Stewart, Robert. 'The Ten Hours and Sugar Crises of 1844: Government and the House of Commons in the Age of Reform', *Historical Journal*, Vol XII, No 1 (1969), 35-57

Thompson, F. M. L. 'Whigs and Liberals in the West Riding', *English Historical Review*, Vol LXXIV (1959), 214-39

Wood, A. C. 'Nottingham, 1835-1865', *Transactions of the Thoroton Society of Nottinghamshire*, Vol LIX (1955), 1-33
Wright, D. G. 'A Radical Borough: Parliamentary Politics in Bradford, 1832-1841', *Northern History*, Vol IV (1969), 132-66

Index